Snakes, Snails,
and
Puppy Dog Tales

A collection of humorous stories about raising boys

Caroline B. Poser

Sand Hill Publications ~ Groton, MA

Snakes, Snails, and Puppy Dog Tales
A collection of humorous stories about raising boys
By Caroline B. Poser

Published by Sand Hill Publications

Illustrations by Lina Liberace, www.linaliberace.com

Cover design and page layout by Kori L. Kennedy, www.mysticdesignco.com

Requests for permission or further information should be addressed to
Sand Hill Publications, P.O. Box 860, Groton, MA 01450

Printed in the United States of America

What are little boys made of?

What are little boys made of?

Snakes and snails

And puppy dog tails,

That's what little boys are made of.

~ Excerpt of an early 19th century nursery rhyme

✒ CONTENTS ✒

❧ INTRODUCTION ❧

"I hope you have a boy!" I had said to my newly pregnant friend as she was holding my infant son. She and her husband already had a little girl.

She had stopped by with her daughter to see our new baby, who was just weeks old, and to bring us some eggs and tomatoes from their chickens and garden. During the visit we had all traipsed up into the boys' room (since they like to show it off, though I have no idea why — it's usually a big mess), where her daughter was fascinated by all the "boy toys" — trucks, building blocks, a couple of race car sets, action figures, and so on. But when she tried to look at any of them with more than her eyes, the boys would reproach her — "That's not for girls!" or "That's mine!" or "Don't touch that!" — and they weren't all that nice about it.

"I don't know how you do it." My friend said as she handed my baby — who had fallen asleep — back to me.

Arranging the baby over my shoulder, I just looked at her, not sure exactly what it was that she didn't know how I did.

"We had my nephew overnight on Saturday" she continued. "He was…" she paused, considering her words carefully, "… a real handful!"

Our ensuing conversation was fragmented, interspersed with, "Be nice, boys," "share your toys with your guest boys," "boys, no yelling, please," and the like.

"Boys and girls are different." We both concluded at the same time, and burst into laughter. I jiggled my dozing son when he startled at our sudden outburst.

It was so true.

I had bought my older boys dolls. First I bought my oldest one because I was about to have a baby and I thought he would want his own "baby." Then I bought my middle son one because his brother had one. Besides, I had grown up with *Free to Be You and Me* and there was a story in that book about a boy who had a doll. I thought it seemed like a good way to help boys learn to be loving and nurturing. However, the most the boys really did with the dolls was push them around in the back of Tonka pick up trucks, or, of course, hit each other with them, or swing them around by one leg before launching them like missiles.

I had brought the dolls with us when we went to the "Big Brother Class" at the hospital when I was seven months pregnant. This was an excruciatingly embarrassing experience as the kids would not sit still for the lesson or activity and literally ran around the room, hid under the tables, darted out the door and down the hall ahead of our tour, and caused mayhem in the maternity ward. One other pregnant mom in the class tried to shield her seemingly shy son from the whirlwind of my two tornadoes — redirecting him as he peered at them timidly — shooting daggers at me while doing so.

My friend and I chatted intermittently as the boys opened their dress-up box, a trunk full of pirate, knight-in-armor, cowboy, and superhero costumes. My friend's daughter stood there with wide eyes. I remembered that I had a tiara in my office and went to get it for her. Upon my return, I saw that the boys had dragged out every imaginable weapon — pistols, swords, daggers, rifles. They began waging a full-scale war with each other, hiding behind chairs, mothers, curtains, and jumping up and down on and in between and over the beds like monkeys.

After my friend admonished one of them for pointing a weapon at her daughter, I wondered if she thought I was cursing her by wishing a boy upon her.

Of course I wasn't. Truthfully, that statement was more about me than it was about my friend. All my life, I had envisioned myself having two children — one of each — like my mom did. With my older two, I didn't know they were boys until they were born. This time around, I'd had amniocentesis and learned ahead of time that I was having another boy. My twinge of disappointment was quickly overshadowed by the fact that the baby was healthy.

Even though I always wanted a daughter — and because my boys can be "a handful" — I wouldn't trade what I've been blessed with for anything.

✖ Crib Notes

I was five nines (99.999%) certain that I had destroyed the crib the night as I tried to put it together single-handedly. I was so sure that I had assembled it by myself the last time, as well as taken it apart. The pieces had been leaning against the wall for at least three weeks, so, I decided on the spur of the moment that evening after dinner and bath to put it together.

The boys had followed me upstairs while I was putting laundry away and started jumping on my bed. I figured that was fine, they needed the exercise. Because of their staggered naps that day, we hadn't spent much time outside, other than the time it took to walk to and from church. Well, I must have been wrong — it quickly became apparent that it was not a project for one.

I asked my oldest if he would come over and hold up one of the side pieces while I screwed it to one of the end pieces. He wouldn't. I asked his brother if he would help me, hoping to leverage competition in my favor. No dice. So. I leaned the pieces on my head as I screwed them together, and then I moved the half crib over against the wall to repeat the process with the other side and end. The real trouble started when I tried to put the two halves together. I couldn't get the pieces to stay in right angles.

Hmmmm. I had the mattress support that hooks into the sides and I figured that if I could get that installed, it would at least keep things squared and I could screw it all together. Well, I couldn't even get two of the hooks in place, and the whole thing collapsed… on me.

By then the boys were very interested in what I was doing, and they came over to "help," which mainly meant playing with all the parts I hadn't used yet, i.e., hardware; using the screwdriver as a microphone; and commandeering the crib mattress as some sort of vehicle. They had already pulled all the pillows and most of the covers off my bed and strewn them on the floor. I asked them again for their help. They declined. So, I told them loudly, "Look, if you're not going to help me, then at least don't bother me! I need the parts back. Now!"

I nearly busted a gut as I wrestled with the pieces. But that wasn't all that was busted. As I tried to line everything up, the sides kept swinging out of control, consequently it became nearly impossible to keep each side bolted to an end, and fully impossible to get the whole thing anywhere near lined up. One by one, little plastic parts started snapping.

At that point, my sons were busy jumping up and down and dancing a naked jig (their bathrobes having been flung aside), and shrieking potty words.

"*Arrrrrgh!*" I growled.

My oldest stopped what he was doing, flopped himself down on my bed, and mimicked my growl. "Mommy, do you *really* have to do that now?" It was an innocent enough question.

I retorted, "Well…do you think…it would be better…for me to do it… with a baby waiting — crying — to go nunnight? *In addition to*…the two of you…jumping-up-and-down-on-my-bed-naked-*and-shrieking!?*"

He looked at me quizzically, silent for a moment. Even though he was somewhat sophisticated at the ripe old age of five, he didn't really understand sarcasm. I felt guilty.

Truthfully, I didn't *have* to do it, I just *wanted to*. I was eight and a half months pregnant and I'd been having Braxton Hicks contractions for a week. I had a rare moment of energy, it wasn't too hot up in the bedroom where the baby would be, and there was just so much to do to get ready, and I was still working full time and planned to until the baby was born! I had been doing an extra load of baby laundry here and there, and now *I really just wanted to put the crib together*.

He ventured, "Well, we want to watch TV!" His brother chimed in, "yeah — we want a show!"

I sighed, "Go then. Go downstairs and turn on the TV."

They didn't want to go by themselves. They went over and sat on the stairs, naked, waiting for me. I took a deep breath and let it out slowly. I leaned the pieces back up against the wall and put the snapped off plastic parts and the remaining hardware back in the Ziploc® baggie on the windowsill.

I got out the porta-crib and put it (unpacked) in the spot next to the changing table, in case the baby came before I figured out what to do about the crib. Then I picked up the boys' bathrobes out of the mess on the floor and escorted them downstairs, turning my back on the project du jour and its aftermath, and turning the Power Rangers on.

I knew that it wouldn't be much longer before our time together would become sporadic and unpredictable, and I might not even be able to watch a whole show with them

❧ Bye For Now, Grandma

It was my last day of maternity leave. My mom had just returned from dropping off the boys at daycare. (Even though the boys and I had been having trial runs for almost the last two weeks, she had taken them that day because my car was at the mechanic's, being looked over to ensure it was ready for commuting the following week.) I asked her how everything went.

"So-and-so was clingy," she replied.

"I'm sure he's sad that you're leaving," I said.

She took off her glasses and wiped her eyes, "He said he wished it was the first day I was here." Her shoulders sagged a bit.

"Oh, I *know!*" I got up and hugged her. I was teary-eyed, too, but didn't want to let the dam overflow just then.

I knew it was going to be hard to say goodbye to my mom. She had been with us all summer, since a week before the baby was born, and now it was time for her to return to her own life in California. I had been trying not to think about this day for a while.

I remembered when she was on her way here — she was driving across the country with her two doggies — when life as we now know it was just beginning.

I could hardly wait for her to arrive. I remembered feeling very nearly insane. I was 38 weeks pregnant, and it was early June. It felt like it was 100 degrees out, even though the thermostat only read 80. I couldn't breathe, I couldn't stand up, I couldn't sit down, I couldn't find the right thing to eat, and it seemed to take me forever to get anything done. I'd been having contractions on and off for a week. Every night, I was afraid that I'd wake up in labor, and be too exhausted to get to the hospital in time. I hadn't been sleeping well and was worn out. Every day my mom called to report on her whereabouts — Nevada, Arizona, New Mexico, Texas, Oklahoma and so on. I could barely manage to work (even though at that point I was working from home), manage kids, and take care of the house.

I remember how relieved I'd been when she called me to say she and the dogs were an hour or so away. Thank God. Then I could relax and enjoy the excitement and the anticipation — the baby could be born at any time. As it turned out, it took him a whole week after my mom got here to make his debut, and she was at the hospital with me when he arrived.

All summer, she helped to manage the older boys so I could tend to the baby (and sometimes she managed the baby so I could tend to the older boys). We went on Friday field trips to museums, farms, and parks, and we even went on vacation together. The boys had grown so attached to her that they started flattering *her* with their worst behavior (usually reserved just for me).

Now this chapter in our lives was coming to an end. My oldest had started kindergarten two days before; my middle son would be starting pre-school the following week; my baby would be starting daycare; I'd be back to work; and Grandma would be gone.

It had actually been the beginning of the end two weeks prior, the day I started the trial runs. I'd cried a few tears on the way home that day, forced to face the fact that this very special, intense, and poignant period of my life would soon be drawing to a close. But I didn't have the luxury of crying that morning as I stood there hugging my mom. I was afraid that if I started, I wouldn't be able to stop.

Even though I wondered how in the world we'd get along without Grandma, I didn't want the boys to know I felt that way. I knew I needed to hold myself together: Mommy's in charge. Mommy's got everything under control. That was the farthest from the truth, but the kids needed to believe it. I could let my guard down later, in private. And then I would turn the page and we would begin living the next chapter of our lives.

I told my mom, "Let's try not to think of it as forever, just 'bye for now.'"

❧ Nuh Uh

Overheard in the car on the way to daycare, a ten-minute ride.

"Nuh uh," My oldest said to his younger brother
"Uh huh," his brother answered
"Nuh uh."
"Uh huh."
"Nuh uh."
"Uh huh."
"Nuh uh!"
"Uh huh!"
"Nuh uh!"
"Uh huh!"
"Nuh uh!"
"Uh huh!"
"Nuh uh!"
"Uh huh!"

The baby startled.
"Boys." I had no idea what they were disagreeing about.

Oldest: "Mmm mm."
Middle: "Mmm hmm."
"Mmm mm."
"Mmm hmm."
"Mmm mm."
"Mmm hmm."
"Mmm mm!"
"Mmm hmm!"
"Mmm mm!"
"Mmm hmm!"
"Mmm mm!"
"Mmm hmm!"

The baby stirred, as their argument gained momentum.
"Boh-oys…" I sang.

Oldest: "No-suh-uh."
Middle: "Yes-suh-uh."
"No-suh-uh."

"Yes-suh-uh."
"No-suh-uh."
"Yes-suh-uh."
"No-suh-uh!"
"Yes-suh-uh!"
"No-suh-uh!!"
"Yes-suh-uh!!"

The baby fussed.
"Boys!" *They* probably had no idea what they were arguing about.

Oldest: "No!"
Middle: "Yes!"
"No!"
"Yes!"
"No!!"
"Yes!!"
"No!!"
"Yes!!"
The baby peeped.
Mommy: "*Boys!* Don't make me stop this car!"

Oldest, quieter: "Nuh uh," he acquiesced, but no doubt emphasizing his position with annoying body language or facial expressions.
Middle, not quieter: "Uh huh!"
Oldest, matching Middle's tone: "Nuh uh!"
Middle, frustrated: "Uh!" whack "huh!!" whack, hitting his brother for emphasis.
Mommy, pulling car into high school parking lot, which was within walking distance from daycare (and in fact, if this had been the 1970's when I was the older kids' age, my mom probably would have told me to get out of the car and hoof it. How times change.): "Oh, no! Unacceptable! That is it! You cannot hit, no matter how frustrated you get!"

Middle: "Hmmmmph!"
Oldest: "*I* didn't hit, Mommy," boasting.
Middle: "Hmmmmph! Fine!" assumes sulking position with arms folded.
Mommy: "Yes However. You have a way of *goading* — uhm — teasing him. It makes him frustrated. You know better. Just. Stop. It! PLEASE!"
Silence, except for Baby's intermittent crying.

"Apologize to each other."
"No!" in unison.
"Apologize!"
Sorry. Sorry. They both muttered.
I fumed and sighed. I was pressed for time.

"Are you ready to go?" I snuck a look into the rear view mirror and saw my oldest smirking, self-satisfied that he could wield this kind of control over his brother.

"Yes, Mommy," they both sighed, exaggeratedly. (Did I detect a note of sarcasm?) No doubt at least one of them rolled his eyes, but I was looking for oncoming traffic, preparing to go the last 100 yards to our destination.

I parked on the side of the building and I let the boys go ahead of me on the sidewalk while I got the baby out of the car. Side by side they walked, continuing their argument.

Oldest: "Nuh uh"
Middle: "Uh huh"
"Nuh uh"
"Uh huh"
"Nuh uh"
"Uh huh"
"Nuh uh"
"Uh huh"

 their voices faded as they approached the front door.

❧ Saying the Pledge of Allegiance

It was a bleak, autumn Monday morning and I was trying to get everyone's gears shifted back to work-school-hurry-up mode. Monday is trash day and I needed to get the kids dropped off at daycare before my weekly 7:30 a.m. conference call.

My then four- and five-year-old sons had been on and off my nerves all weekend. In between the art projects, games, stories, chores, trip to the supermarket, and trying to maintain reverence in church was a generous helping of hitting, kicking, throwing things, waking the baby up, jumping on the furniture, mimicking, and backtalk. I didn't feel all that well-rested.

I had to make multiple trips in and out of the house carrying the trash and recycling and gathering all the various and sundry supplies we need for a day at daycare and school and work — blankets for nap time, lunches and formula, my briefcase and laptop — not to mention the baby, who I had carried out and tucked into his car seat.

Each time I trudged in and out of the house I found it necessary to encourage the boys, who had made it as far as the porch, to continue moving towards the door and out to the car.

"Put your shoes on, please.
"Have you got those shoes on yet?"
"Boys, what did Mommy ask you?"
"Do you need some help with those shoes?"

On my last trip, I caught both of them goofing around in front of the house, jumping up and down, trying to touch the flag that was swaying in the chilly breeze. We'd been flying the American flag since September 11, 2001.

Exasperated, I sputtered, "BOYS! Why.Aren't.You.In.The.Car.Yet!"

Two sets of angelic eyes — one brown, one blue — turned to look at me like I was stupid.

"We're gonna say the Pledge of Allegiance!" (The oldest had just learned it in school and was teaching it to his younger brother.)

Oh, of course — silly me. With a long sigh, I felt my annoyance dissipating, and my heart swelling with pride — not just for my boys but for the symbol of our nation. "Oh. Well…that's a good idea. I know, let's all say it!" And I placed my hand over my heart.

My five year old smiled at me quizzically, "How do *you* know the Pledge of Allegiance, Mommy!?"

ꝍ Hairum-Scarum

I decided I should buy a hair clipper set so I could cut the boys' hair myself. I'd been thinking about it for a while, and when I saw one on Drugstore.com for just a little more than the price of one boy's hair cut, I added it to my online shopping cart.

I had wanted to go to hair dressing school after high school, but that was not an option in my family. So I went to college, and became president of "Beauty Workshop" where I cut and styled my friends' hair. Sometimes they even paid me.

My thwarted desire to be a hairdresser was not the reason that I bought the clipper set, however. Avoiding either the ordeal of hauling three boys into the local barbershop where patrons were served in the order in which they walked in (which meant we risked a long wait) or the embarrassment I faced when they ran amok and were unable to keep their hands off the displays in the salon where I went were my primary motivators.

Additionally, the idea of saving $30+ a month plus the trip to Dunkin' Donuts afterwards (because it is right next to the barber shop in town), was appealing, as was the fact that if I did it myself, I could do it anytime.

The clipper set sat in its box for a couple of weeks after I bought it because I did not have the energy to unpack it and read the instructions, nor did I want to perform my first hair cuts prior to picture day at school.

Then one Saturday when I'd just put the baby back to bed for his morning nap, and the The big boys, a.k.a., "The Bigs," had already had too much TV by 8:00 a.m., I said, "Hey, let's figure out how to use this thing!"

They were all too ready to help me tear open the package and inventory the pieces. Anything involving blades and scissors is just great with them.

In retrospect, I should have done that part by myself. As I was sorting through all the attachments, the boys took off with the actual clippers and plugged them in. *Buzzzzzzzzzzz!*

"No, no, no, boys! Wait for Mommy." *No time like the present,* I figured.

"Who's first?" Wrong question. That started an argument.

I picked my oldest. I figured he'd follow my directions better, maybe even sit still.

Actually using the clippers was easy, and kind of fun, but I wished I'd taken the time to either read the instructions or watch the little DVD. I wondered if I'd chosen the right attachment when my son's scalp became immediately visible. I could have started long and gone shorter, but not vice versa. However, I was committed. Hair was flying all over the place. My middle son was dancing through it (making a general nuisance of himself, irked that he hadn't gone first), and I could hear the baby on the monitor (he was teething and couldn't make up his mind about whether to fish or cut bait regarding either napping or eating lately). I wasn't exactly sure how to do the hairline part. When I said as much, my son told me, "You're doing fine, Mommy. That's just how the barber does it."

When he started complaining that he itched and had hair in his mouth, I unwrapped the towel from around his neck and pronounced him done. He got up and shook himself off. "Wait," I said, eyeing him critically. "Let me just tidy up this part."

So he stood there, squirming and shuddering and griping about the hair all over him, as I made the daring move of clipping with no attachments (that's as short as it gets) around his ears and the nape of his neck, with his brother circling around us, ricocheting off kitchen appliances. All of a sudden, my oldest hauled off and delivered one of his special customized karate kicks at his brother, causing the clippers to swerve. *Oh, no!* I thought, and may have even said that out loud. *I didn't want to have to go to the barber after all this!*

"Hold still, please!" I ordered. I knew I had to wrap it up. I wondered if anyone would tease him about his not-quite-professional hair cut. "Okay, honey, you're good. I'm not sure I'm as good as the barber…but you look handsome!"

He went into the bathroom and climbed up onto the sink so he could see in the mirror. "I like it, Mommy," he assured me. "It's a good job for your first time!"

❧ Birthday Party Mad Lib

The _____ (adjective) day had finally arrived — _____ (name of child)'s birthday! S/he had been _____ (adverb) counting down the days for weeks. S/he could barely wait for the _____ (adjective) party when all his/her _____ (adjective) friends would be there to celebrate. _____ (name of child) was a/an _____ (adjective) _____ (number) -year-old _____ (type of animal) already.

His/her Mommy could hardly believe it. It seemed like just yesterday when s/he was a _____ (adjective), _____ (adjective) baby. The years had flown by so _____! (adverb)

There was a time when (name of child) couldn't _____ (verb) or _____ (verb) and now s/he was _____ing (verb) and _____ing (verb) like all the other _____ (adjective) _____ (plural noun) in his/her class.

_____ (name of child) was grateful that he had such _____ (adjective) friends who brought him all sorts of really _____ (adjective) gifts for his birthday. He thought, *"Being _____ (same number as above) is pretty cool!"*

❧ Playing Games

"Mommy, can we play a game?" My oldest asked me as I was jiggling and rocking the baby in one arm, and simultaneously trying to hang onto his "lovey," the teddy bear-blanket combo that he has snuggled since birth, and wrestle the nipple part of his "baba" into place with my free hand, during which time he was groping, writhing, arching his back, crying, and yanking my hair. My middle son, a.k.a. the whirling dervish, was dancing to some rhythm that only he could hear, orbiting around us as I shuffled from the kitchen towards the upstairs.

"Not right this minute" I answered gruffly.

He drooped a little. Lately he had been reminding me, "You *always do everything* for the baby!" Which of course is true, the baby can't do anything for himself, and even though I reminded him that I did everything for him — and his next younger brother, too — when they were babies, I'm sure that didn't do much to ease his current Mommy-deficit.

"I'm sorry, honey," I sighed. "Just let me just get the baby settled."

The baby was overtired. He had learned to crawl two weeks before — if you could call that scooting thing he did (alternating one knee and the opposite buttock) "crawling" — and was starting to pull up. He couldn't seem to stop himself from practicing his new skills. I had tried to put him to bed a half an hour earlier, but he had apparently got into a kneeling-and-shaking-the-side-of-the-crib position and couldn't stop — the polar opposite of "I've fallen and can't get up."

I managed to tuck him back into bed and coo at him over his noisy crying, "Nunnight, my love. You must be so tired. Mommy can see that you are so tired. Get some rest. Mommy will see you later. Mommy loves you." I walked out with the baba that he refused, tucking my hair back into place and reorganizing myself to face the next-most-immediate concern, The Game.

I knew my son wouldn't let me forget. And I didn't really want to, except for the fact that it's nearly impossible to play a game with both of my older boys. My oldest likes to play chess and checkers and other board games like Parcheesi. His brother just isn't there yet. Now that I think of it, he doesn't really like card games either, and my oldest has progressed far beyond War (thank God) and has been playing Uno for quite a while.

I put my housework blinders on to help me ignore the pile of dishes in the sink and on the counters, and all the laundry that needed to be gathered from the backs of the dining room chairs, the rest stop on its journey between sitting in the laundry basket and being folded. I sat down on the couch with the boys.

What we wound up doing was playing "I Spy." Perfect because the rules are very simple and there are no pieces anyone can sweep off the board in frustration. And since we were sitting in the living room, it ought to be a breeze compared to where we usually played, which was in the car. Because unless we were spying things in the car (which makes for a very fast game), we'd usually driven past whatever I-Spy spied, making it impossible to guess.

I let my oldest go first. He spied something green. His brother got so excited about guessing, I couldn't get a word in edgewise, which was okay. My oldest had cleverly picked something that was not obvious to either his brother or me. When his brother started getting annoyed, I made some guesses. I finally guessed the numbers on the cable box. It figures he had his eyes glued to the TV, even though it wasn't on! I let my other son take my turn, since he'd put most of the detective work into it.

Staring straight at his blue water bottle, he said, "I thpy with my widdo eye…thumthing bwoo!"

"That's easy!" his brother exclaimed triumphantly. "It's your water bottle!"

"Awwwww!" my middle son groaned and threw himself on the couch, folding his arms and knitting his eyebrows together.

My oldest made gloating noises.

I glared at him, and tried to keep my voice light, "Okay, honey, let's let your brother go again. And to my middle son, "Come here. Mommy wants to tell you a secret."

I explained to him that he should decide on the thing that he I-thpied and keep looking around the room before he gave the clue. His eyes widened, and then he squinted as the light bulb went on. I could imagine the gears turning in his head. He thpied something red, and it took his brother a lot of guesses before he got it, and subsequently wanted to know the secret.

My oldest then spied an obscure and tiny detail on one of the baby toys and we all got bored with the game before anyone guessed it.

Our next game was *Guess Who?*, where two players try to deduce the identity of their opponent's "Mystery Person," using game boards with 48 frames apiece and an equal number of cards displaying character faces. Players ask one another yes or no questions that help narrow the pool of possibilities. My oldest didn't want to play, probably because his brother is an equal match for him. The boys set up the game on the floor and played each other while I helped them ask the right questions, i.e., don't ask "does your person have brown eyes" if they've just determined that the person's eyes aren't blue and don't ask if the person is bald if you know it's a woman.

My oldest won the first game. I convinced his brother they should do a "best out of three" tournament. I said to my middle son, "I'll be on your team, if you want, honey." He said, "I know, 'Boys against Mommy!'" He turned on me (which was not unusual)! I joined them on the floor and we played a couple more games. They won the first, lorded it over me for a while, and the second one was a bust as I 'fessed up when I realized I could see who their secret person was when a ray of mid-afternoon sunlight light shone through the card just the right way.

Tired of *Guess Who?*, we moved on to *Trouble*, a board game with a simple concept: to be the first player to send four game pieces all the way around the board, moving spaces determined by rolls of the dice. The "trouble" comes when an opponent's piece lands on an already-occupied space, thus sending the first piece back to the beginning.

Truthfully, I was tired of sitting on the hardwood floor and playing games for ages 3-6, but I couldn't let on. At least the TV wasn't on, at least the boys were practicing taking turns and cooperating, at least the baby was napping, affording me the opportunity to spend quality time with the The Bigs, I consoled myself.

Trouble is not my favorite game. It turned out to be the general consensus by the time we were done, too. My middle son got stuck in home and couldn't pop a six to get out, and he got more and more frustrated. It was hard for him to contain himself from slamming the Pop-o-matic and he got so annoyed he covered his eyes before each whack, unable to bear the sight of any number that wasn't a six. I was stuck in home, too, and my oldest was merrily circling the board, effectively playing by himself, sure he was going to win, and unable to keep that fact to himself.

Finally, I popped a six and told my middle son he could take it. Surprisingly, he did not refuse my offer, as I knew his rules-based brother would have, and took the free pass. Equally surprising was the fact that his older brother didn't make a stink about it.

After a lengthy game and cliff-hanging turn of events, my oldest ended up in tears as his brother traipsed off while doing the happy dance because he had beat me by one space, while his brother was stuck in home. Now my oldest took the opportunity in between sobs to tell me that I was a cheater for giving away the six. I agreed that it was kind of like cheating, but it was the only way we were going to be able to finish the game, and "Mommy is grateful to have such a big boy who understands these things, and oh-by-the-way, please don't mention that to your brother." As I shoved all the pieces back into the box, I could hear the baby stirring over the monitor.

I creaked to my feet and helped my oldest up. I gave him a squeeze and kissed his head. Then I put the games away, making sure to find a nice out-of-the-way spot for Trouble behind the puzzles on the game shelf in the living room. Game over.

❧ What Mommy Says and What They Hear: Our Morning Routine

What Mommy Says: "Boys, it's time to get ready for school. Bring your dishes into the kitchen please, and let's get your teeth brushed."
What They Hear: "Boys, show Mommy how you can balance a plate on your head, swordfight with your forks, and dance a jig while holding your crotch."

WMS: "Uhm…boys…does either of you need to go potty before we get into the car?"
WTH: "Boys, why don't you see if you can both peepee at the same time without getting any on the toilet or the floor or each other."

WMS: "Did you wash your hands, boys?"
WTH: "Boys, why not squirt soap all over each other?"

WMS: "Here are your lunch boxes — can you put them in your backpacks, please?"
WTH: "Wander around the house and seek out things you can cram into your backpacks. Don't forget your stuffed animals, super hero action figures, and the monster trucks that Grandma sent for Christmas. Did you get your art supplies, in case they don't have any at school today? Okay, good, now you can yell at me because you can't fit your lunch box into your backpacks, please."

WMS: I know you went potty, but did you brush your teeth, boys?
WTH: Boys, run upstairs and get your Hot Wheels toothbrush because I know you certainly must be tired of using the Power Rangers one like you have been every-other-morning-for-the-past-three-months! Don't forget the detour into your bedroom to practice juggling and visit with your weapons collection, since you can't bring any of it to school."

WMS: "Okay — good job on those teeth."
WTH: "Okay — climb up on the sink so you can admire your teeth in the mirror. Push and shove until one of you falls into the bathtub."

WMS: "Alrighty…let's get those coats and shoes on, boys."
WTH: "Boys, go ahead and have a shoe fight while trying to figure out whose shoes are whose. Never mind your little brother or the window or any other fragile thing in your path."

WMS: "Okay, okay! Enough! Just.Go.Out.The.Door. Your brother and I are right behind you!"
WTH: "Okay, okay! Shuffle your feet and bounce off the porch walls and each other on the way out to the driveway. Try to squeeze through the door at the same time. Drop your backpacks in the big puddle next to the car. Then hide! Hide! Hide! Quick!

WMS: "C'mon, boys! I don't want to be late for work!"
WTH: "C'mon boys! I'm always late for work!" (I know they think this because I overheard one of them tell his teacher, "Mommy's always late for work," which is not true, you can ask my manager.)

WMS: "Phew. Finally! Boys, what do you think we could do to make it easier to get out the door in the morning?"
WTH:

❧ The Most Magical Place on Earth

I had parked the stroller right near Cinderella's castle. Grandma and my four-year-old were in a nearby rest room going potty before we left The Magic Kingdom, a.k.a. "The Most Magical Place on Earth," for the day. I was trying to keep my eye on my six-year-old, who was twirling around a nearby post. Because I had schlepped a heavy backpack, as well as my nine-month-old in a front pack, my back and shoulders were tired. I had shrugged the back-pack off and the baby was ensconced in the stroller, having a nap.

"Oh, not again!" I moaned as I bent over to retrieve something out of the huge carry-almost-all pack. Groping blindly, I felt that the contents were slimy.

I withdrew my hand and examined it. It was covered with an orange-ish ooze, which meant that not only had the little tub of cheese crackers opened up inside the pack, but somehow there was liquid involved.

It was ninety-something degrees: we were in the middle of a Florida heat wave in April. This ooze was smeared all over the contents of the pack, which was nearly everything we'd brought into the park, which is signifi-cant when you have to carry supplies for three children. "Oh, gross!" I shuddered, as I realized this was no doubt a contributing factor to the clammy feeling on my back. My son came trotting over, drawn as a moth to a flame to anything yucky.

A woman in a wheel chair nearby asked me, "Are we having fun yet?" I realized she had been watching me fumble, and probably witnessed my expression morph from surprise to disgust to annoyance.

Not feeling very "magical" at that moment, I replied, "It's been a long day. I'm just ready to go home." I didn't want to say anything snippy in front of my son, who had attached himself to me, peering at the woman cautiously.

"That's why I don't have kids," she scowled, and proceeded to sit there and watch me taking stock of the mess in the backpack, removing items one by one.

I gasped, and turned to my son. "Honey, do you need a drink?" I gave his water bottle a quick clean up with a baby wipe before I handed it to him.

"Thank you, mama." He was now holding on to the stroller where the baby slept, protectively.

She continued, "How many more days do you have?" as if it were a prison sentence.

I told her, "Two more days," and didn't reciprocate the question to her. I didn't really want to be having a conversation with her at all. I knew that there was no way I'd be able to explain to her why I had come to Disney World with my children, if she was of the ilk that chose not to have children.

Raising kids is not a predictable or tidy thing to do, and it was unfortunate that this woman had seen one of the more challenging moments involved in parenting, for it only served to validate her opinion that having kids was a job, not a joy. What she didn't get to see was that there are a lot of fun parts, too — that I get to sing and play and rediscover the world through new eyes. And ultimately I get to experience the true meaning of unconditional love, to feel the love of God pouring through me to my children, and then reflected back from them. The "Most Magical Place on Earth" is wherever my kids are.

I had been planning to surprise the boys with the trip for months — mostly so I did not have to endure weeks of them asking "how many more days until…" (We can barely get through the morning of a birthday party day without them asking every ten or fifteen minutes, "how much longer to so-and-so's party.").

On Easter, Grandma and I put clues in some of the The Bigs' Easter eggs — pictures of the entrance to the Magic Kingdom and of Mickey Mouse. Watching them as they realized that we were actually going to Disney World and that we were leaving *that very day* was a joy in itself. "Pack your bags, boys!" I told them, and we were on the plane five hours later, headed for eight jam-packed days full of excitement with just a touch of vomit, potty accidents, bickering, and overtired children who for some reason can't get to sleep at night.

Of course I was ready for a vacation after we returned from our family vacation. But it's all worthwhile when I hear the kids tell God, even years later, "and thank you for the time we went to Disney World" when they say their prayers.

✢ Heaven

Chatting about the day as I tucked my older boys in, I said, "Boys, I wanted to let you know that Grandma's dog died today."

"She did?" my oldest answered.

"Yes. I'm really sorry to have to tell you that."

"At least she had her birthday." And it was true. Her birthday was the day that Grandma had her euthanized. "How did it happen?"

"Well, Grandma took her to the veterinarian, and the vet gave her some medicine, and then she died."

"Why did she need medicine? She didn't feel good?"

"No, honey, she was old and sick. Remember last weekend when she couldn't stop throwing up? She just wasn't herself anymore. She couldn't eat, and didn't want to play; she didn't even want to sit with Grandma on the couch. Dying happens to everyone someday…"

"I don't want to die."

"I don't want you to, either. But I don't think it's the end of everything. It's just the end of life here. Don't forget about heaven…" I thought about something a friend of mine had quipped, "Everyone wants to go to heaven but no one wants to die to get there."

"I wonder what heaven is like?"

"Well, I don't really know…" *and I don't even know exactly where it is, either,* I thought, recalling a conversation the kids and I'd had at dinner one night when my five-year-old was using the placemat with the map of the United States on it. He could recognize certain states like California, Texas, New York, Florida, and Massachusetts, and then he'd asked me, "Where's Heaven?"

I had tried not to laugh out loud, but was unsuccessful.

His older brother had answered, "Heaven's up in the sky, where God is!"

I had let it go at that. Why complicate things?

Probably recalling the same dinner conversation, my hiding-under-his-covers, silent-up-until-then-five-year-old-answered, "Well, God is there."

"That's right. And Jesus, too," his brother added.

"I think heaven is better than we can even imagine now — maybe it will be like 100 Disney Worlds," I offered, using an example that the kids could relate to. "Or a thousand. Or a million!"

"Maybe it will be a chocolate world!" My younger son popped out from under his covers and sat up in bed.

"Maybe it will be all kids and no bosses!" his older brother said.

Hmmm, I thought, *no bosses?* I reflected upon my corporate life.

"Yeah! No teachers. No one to tell us what to do. All kids."

"Except we'd want to see you there, Mommy…"

"I hope they have TV in Heaven."

"Well, if heaven is all that much better than anything we can imagine, then your heaven will probably have TVs everywhere."

"And chocolate," my younger son reminded us.

"And my heaven will be 100 Disney Worlds!" My oldest chimed in. "And you can come to my heaven, Mommy. And you, too, he said to his brother."

"Oh, thanks, honey!" I replied. And as I considered being together with my children for all eternity, I was grateful to know that there are many rooms in heaven.

✥ Momorabilia

I was standing in the school office, signing out after a shift of helping in my oldest son's class, chatting with the three office ladies. One of them was leafing through a stack of spiral bound books, which reminded me that I'd had a question about the Memory Books that had been advertised in a take home flyer.

"Are those samples of the Memory Books? You know the ones the PTA is offering?"

"Oh, no, these are day planners. The third and fourth graders use them."

Eyebrows raised, I said, "Wow — they're probably more organized than I am!"

The ladies chuckled. *Did that mean they were equally unorganized?*

I continued, "Well, I just wondered about the Memory Books, do you think it's the kind of thing I should get one of, to share, between my two kids, or would they each want their own?"

One of the ladies said, "Well, they might each want one…"

"Well, I can imagine they might, if they were in high school, but they're only in kindergarten and first…"

Another added, "Well…you don't want them fighting over it when they're grown up…"

"…and they're boys." I added.

All three said simultaneously, "Oh, they won't care."

"Yeah, I didn't really think so."

Then I confessed to the ladies about how I'd given up on scrapbooking and even thrown out the baby books. I just couldn't keep up after I'd had my third son. I had been drowning in memorabilia and it was just such a relief to get rid of it.

For several years I had simply shoved sticky notes, random artwork, class photos, progress reports, and the like in a drawer in a filing cabinet in my office (not filed, just stuck in the drawer). The drawer had become full, and the resulting pile on top of the filing cabinet was precarious. After adding another baby to our family, I'd started thinking reluctantly about taking stock of all this stuff. I thought I should make sure to save all the equivalent things for him (in a similar keepsake box) with a comparable baby book so I could keep track of the same milestones.

I'd soon realized my logic was flawed.

First of all, my boys don't care about equivalent or similar. It's only fair if things are exactly 100% equal. The same. And even then, sometimes it's "not fair" ("That's not the one I had." "How do you know?" "I just know. I want the one he has!" "I can't see a difference." "There is. I want his.")

Secondly, it is highly doubtful that these boys are going to care about this stuff at all, not now and certainly not in 20 years.

I thought about life 20 years down the road. If none of this stuff mattered to the boys, would I be grateful that I had charted, documented, collected, collated, packaged, and carted all of the memorabilia around for their whole lifetimes?

I doubted it.

It had been a tremendous enough burden trying to remember to do everything equally for The Bigs. Recreating it all for the baby would have put me over the edge. I didn't get off to a great start. Most of the pictures I had taken after he was born were of my middle son's birthday party and our excursions to a museum, a farm, and a park. Yes, the baby had joined us, but since his backdrop was usually his car seat, I didn't take too many pictures of him. Everyone says the second child gets short-changed as far as photographs. Because The Bigs were so close together, I made sure that didn't happen. However, the theory had proven true for my third within six weeks.

The more I thought about it, the more I realized I didn't care what the baby wore home from the hospital or when a tooth came in or who gave what baby gifts. And I knew that if I didn't have anything to paste in to a certain area, like an ultrasound picture or a newspaper announcement, that the blank spots would haunt me.

I thought about another mom I knew whose second son, upon discovery that his older brother had a baby book, asked his mom where his was. She told him she'd look for it in the attic while he was in school the next day. That day, instead of going to the attic, she went to the store and bought a baby book and spent the entire day fabricating everything. That could be me. And though doing that would likely be less painful than keeping up and keeping things equal for the next 20 years, not doing it at all would be even more desirable. So I got rid of everyone's baby books, including he baby's brand new book that still had its plastic cover on it. The only sticky notes I had for him were, "first smile, first bath, cut nails, first bottle, found thumb (aside from eat, poop, cry, and sleep, that summed up his life history: he was only six weeks old).

I felt a tremendous wave of relief when I decided to let go of documenting the details of the lifetimes of my three children.

❧ The Young and the Restless

4:02 a.m. wake-up call: crying baby. On autopilot, I shuffled down to my youngest son's room and took him out of his crib. Dear God, *please* don't make me get up now…

"Ah-stee-ahz?" he whimpered.

"Oh, no no no no no. Baby, it's still nunnight!" *And it's Sunday*, I thought. Any attempt to convince him would be futile: he just wanted to go downstairs.

"Ah-stee-ahz!" he insisted, beginning to sob again.

"Oh, honey," I wailed. "Mommy's still tie-tie!"

Resigned to my fate, I carried him down to the living room, plunked him on the love seat with a pillow and blanket, and continued on to the kitchen.

"Baba?"

"Yes, honey, baba."

Momentarily, I made my way back with the bottle and handed it to him.

"Tee tyoo," he sang.

"You're welcome." I sighed and sunk into the other couch, curling up with my own pillow and blanket. I did not turn on any lights.

We vegged in each other's general direction. When he finished his bottle, he slid off his couch wordlessly and cruised over to mine.

I helped him up and he laid his head on the pillow I'd been leaning on. I covered him with my blanket. Then he proceeded to wiggle and squirm and scratch me with his little toenails. Eventually, he slept and I dozed about as comfortably as if I were on a red-eye flight.

At 5:15 or so, my middle son came downstairs. We did not speak. I pointed to the love seat and tossed him another pillow and he actually covered his own self up with the blanket his brother had abandoned.

I reached out with the arm that wasn't holding the baby on the couch and we held hands companionably.

Sometime later, my oldest son came down and draped himself on top of my body, carefully avoiding the baby.

"Mommy," he said. "It's time to get up!"

"No, it isn't honey," I whispered. "We're still sleeping."

"But Mommy, it's five-four-four!"

"That's okay, honey. It's Sunday. We don't have to go anywhere until church."

Silence.

"But I want to get up." Twitch.
"Go ahead, honey."
Twitch, fidget.
"Hold still please."
Temporary stillness, then…
Twitch, fidget, nudge.
"Stop!" I hissed.
Twitch, fidget, nudge, scratch.
"Please!" I poked him.
Twitch, fidget, nudge, scratch, sniff.
"Go ahead, honey, puh-LEEZ! Just go get a Go-GURT® *and… watchTVin-myroom!*
"But Mommy…" Whine. Wiggle, writhe.
"Shhh! Just go!" I gave him an encouraging prod.

By that time his brother had awakened and said perkily, "I'll watch TV with you!" and off they went. Mercifully, the baby remained sleeping. Why my children get up before it's light out on weekends and need to be dragged out of bed at six-five-nine — or later — on school days is beyond me.

At least we'd have plenty of time to get ready for church, I thought as I closed my eyes again, ascribing to the sleep-while-the-baby-sleeps philosophy. After all, it was not yet 6:00 a.m. And it was Sunday.

❧ Boy to the World!

How was your weekend?" the daycare office manager asked me.

"Not that great," I replied with a sigh. It was first thing Monday morning.

Raised eyebrows.

"My children are like a small band of monkeys." (At the time my three boys were six and under).

"Oh, well…it's that time of year…"

"I suppose…"

I was recovering from the second weekend in Advent.

I had arranged my work schedule and decreased my commitments in an effort to *enjoy* the holiday season that year. But it wasn't happening.

I had envisioned that the kids and I would put up the tree and decorate it during Thanksgiving weekend while listening to Christmas music. Then over the course of the next several weeks, we'd bake cookies, and make peppermint bark and other treats together, including our traditional gingerbread structures. We'd talk about the story of Jesus' birth while we set up our nativity scene under the tree. We'd watch some Christmas movies, make wish lists for Santa, and observe Advent every Sunday. That meant I'd have to plan a lesson and an activity and a treat, but that would be okay. After all, I was only working four-day weeks in December. We'd count down the days with our Advent calendar. Yeah, right.

What it was really like in my house…

I put up the tree. The boys lost interest in decorating it after hanging a few ornaments each, after which they proceeded to use them as missiles and other weapons. A couple of weeks later, our tree was mostly decorated on the top half, as is the tree of any family that includes an eighteen-month old. (Though, one day I *did* find a pair of dirty socks draped across some of the lower branches.)

The boys would have rather watched Power Rangers reruns than any of my favorite Christmas specials like "Santa Claus is Comin' to Town," "Rudolph the Red-Nosed Reindeer," or "Frosty The Snowman." I insisted they do that upstairs. So much for togetherness.

Creating our gingerbread house was extravagantly messy affair. Not only because the pastry bag sprung a few leaks but also because I can never keep those things twisted closed, and the icing always squeezes out the back way, we all used our hands to smear the royal icing "mortar" on the gingerbread pieces before we stuck them together. It was decimated nearly as soon as it was built. The kids picked the candy off of it and then the older two reduced it to rubble with their fists. And more than a week later, I was still finding crusted icing on various knobs, dials, switches, and faucets.

I considered briefly the "Pajama Run," an event one of my colleagues includes in her holiday celebration, which consists of driving around in your PJs with hot cocoa to look at Christmas lights. I discarded it just as quickly. Until someone invents soundproof, Plexiglas® units that fit over booster seats, we'll observe holiday lights on our regular, utilitarian routes. My youngest was just as happy to look at the "moom."

Speaking of my youngest, he couldn't keep his hands off the electronics and quashed every single Christmas CD I put on. Because I play them in the DVD player attached to the TV, he couldn't understand why there's sound, but no picture. "Show?" he would ask plaintively as he handed me the fingerprint-covered CD he'd just divested from the DVD player. So much for the Christmas music.

Instead, I was frequently serenaded by the older boys belting out "Jingle bells, Batman smells, the Joker learned ballet…hee hee hee snicker snicker snort!" Another very special musical number was "Who Let the Dogs Out?" rendered on percussion instruments.

The older boys fought over the Advent calendar. My oldest figured out if he was odds, then he'd not only get more days, but he'd get *the day*. My youngest wasn't participating in this yet other than to examine and then discard on the floor every day's felt-and-Velcro® nativity-scene characters, much to the chagrin of the two rules-based, school-aged kids, who tried in vain to keep the characters in sequential order beginning with the star, angel, and shepherds and ending with the wisemen, gifts, and Jesus. When I moved the calendar upstairs into the The Bigs' room, we lost count. Oh, well.

I was on overload, as I was essentially trying to cram five days worth of work into four days on top of all the added holiday hoopla. This resulted in my sampling far too many cookies and chocolates, and drinking too much coffee. And I won't go into detail about why I needed to replace both my laptop and cell phone within a two week period, but suffice it to say that the loss of data was a major setback for me.

The The Bigs made a battle scene out of the nativity set and launched baby Jesus off the roof of the crèche. That we still had tiny baby Jesus and his little straw bed after four seasons was, in itself, one of the miracles of Christmas. Compounding their irreverence was the extent of their interest in our Advent celebration. "Fire. Heh-Heh. Heh-Heh. That's cool," about summed it up.

"It's chaos at my house," I concluded to the office manager.

"C'mon, that's all part of the fun!" she chuckled and nudged me.

I rolled my eyes. "Uh huh."

But, as I drove off that morning, I thought a lot about our conversation. I really didn't want to be such a grinch, and the office manager was right — this *was* Christmas — all the boys' antics should be taken in stride, because it really was all part of the fun. Right then and there, I decided to embrace the pandemonium.

The rest of the holiday season included my youngest's new tradition of pulling pine cones, bells, and candy canes off the tree (the only things left on the bottom half) and hiding them around the house and The Bigs' regular habit of shrieking potty words and scrapping like a couple of puppies. I knew that reminders of Santa Claus seeing them when they're sleeping, knowing when they're awake, knowing if they've been bad or good would be in vain. So, I simply told them I expected the mess to be cleaned up before they watched their superhero cartoons.

My children's gift to me was to remind me to view Christmas as they do. Once I aligned my vision with reality, I was fully able to enjoy the season. And pinecones, bells, and candy canes continued to surface until Easter.

Boy to the world!

❧ Out with the Old

"That's okay — we can just buy another one," my five-year-old said after he broke one of his older brother's Christmas gifts.

"Not so fast!" I said. "That was a very special gift from Santa! Who do you think is going to 'just buy another one'?"

"Well…you are, Mommy." He looked at me like I was stupid.

"I don't *think* so!" I huffed.

I don't know how much of this was his wishful thinking — I am sure he felt bad he had destroyed his brother's PlayTV Baseball, and I wondered how 'accidental' it was: he sometimes morphed into the Tasmanian Devil when frustrated — and how much was a case of "I-have-too-much-and-nothing-is-sacred-itis," also known as "affluenza," according to Grandma.

It was Christmas afternoon.

I vowed that before the week was up, I'd clean out the The Bigs' room. It was something I should have done prior to the onslaught of all the Christmas gifts.

It became especially evident during that week between Christmas and New Year's that there was just too much stuff in our snug house. The boys and all their accessories were all over the place, bouncing off the walls, furniture, and each other. Every time I walked through the living room, I had to shuffle my way through the pillows and blankets from the couches, toys, and games — many of them electronic — and often the boys themselves, who were literally underfoot as they wrestled and rolled around on the floor, juice cups, babas, and snack bowls teetering precariously amongst the overflow from the coffee and end tables.

Asking the boys to clean their room was futile, since all they did was shove stuff in drawers and on shelves or in the closet. If I cleaned their room, I could purge. I could get rid of all the fast food children's meal toys and trinkets and trash that had accumulated from goody bags and moments of weakness (mine) when we passed vending machines in the supermarket or bowling alley.

This had been hard for me in the past because there might be that once-in-a-blue-moon moment where one of them would recall something they once had, which was all of a sudden the most important thing in the world, their prized possession.

Like the Sponge Bob plug-n-play video game.

There was one time that my oldest became obsessed with finding a Sponge Bob video game. Unfortunately for him, I had put in the recycle bin at the supermarket months earlier when he became seriously in-volved with his Game Boy.

"I really want to play with that video game." *Uh oh…*

"I'm sure we don't have that anymore, honey."

Pause.

"All I really want to do is play with that video game."

"I don't know where it is, honey." *Technically true. I know where I put it, but have no idea where it went from there.*

"The game in my Game Boy is too hard!"

"Do you want me to help you read the words?"

"No. I really want to play with that video game. I haven't played it in a long time!"

"Last time you played it you got mad, remember?"

"I know it's in the closet upstairs! Why can't I just look!?" *Because this is where I stash your Easter eggs, extra birthday presents that I keep on hand, the special Christmas wrapping paper from Santa Claus…stuff I don't want you to see.*

"Okay. Fine, go ahead — I'm sure you won't find it." And, coward that I was, I let him, knowing he wasn't going to take my word for it, and hop-ing that the items I didn't want him to see were suitably camouflaged. Fortunately, before he got too far into the "closet," which is actually the eaves of the attic, he found something else that distracted us from the quest for Sponge Bob.

Though we'd talked about wants versus needs, and I'd only just recently relayed a magazine article I'd read about homeless kids and what they wanted for Christmas — stuff my boys took for granted: a bed, a house, a car, friends, I knew that the boys' case of affluenza was nobody's fault but mine.

Fueled by the thought, I got started on their room. I took all the action figures — Bible Man, Bat Man, Red Power Ranger (two of those), and assorted villains and sidekicks and put them and all their weapons and other trappings aside in a big zippered freezer bag — a veritable treasure trove for someone who would appreciate them. My boys hadn't been playing with them and besides one of them got the Power Rangers Mystic Force Megazord from Santa, which is made up of five individual Power Rangers, so it's not like their lives are devoid of action figures.

I thinned out the Halloween costumes, removing the cracked masks and things too creepy to pass down to the youngest. Maybe he'd want to be — was that Wolverine? — when he turned five, but I'd worry about that when the time came.

I sorted through multitudes of bouncy balls, el-cheapo yoyos, mini flying discs, and other piñata-filler-quality plastic items. I liberated all the LEGO® sets from their individual plastic baggies and tossed them into the bin (sans packaging or instructions) with the vintage LEGOs we'd bought at our neighbor's yard sale. These were the good, old-fashioned LEGOs that can make anything you can imagine, not just specific vehicles, Bionicles®, or Exo-Force® robots. And I got rid of an entire race car set that we'd bought at a church fair and wasn't even all there to begin with. I was ruthless. And when all was said and done, I'd put together eight or so bags to either throw out or put in the recycle bin.

And then I began my promotional campaign to encourage them to migrate themselves and their things out of the living room.

"Look boys, Mommy cleaned your room — now you have space to play up here! Isn't that great!?" (wink wink, nudge nudge.)

"Boys, why don't you go play with your new Hot Wheels® set — in your room?"

"Boys, stop roughhousing in the living room! You can take that behavior outside or *up to your room!*"

A week went by, then a month, and even now, years later, no one has ever asked for anything that was removed from their room.

Regarding the PlayTV Baseball game, rather than just buy another one, we had the original one fixed. And I could hear the boys playing with it much more reverently than before…in their room.

❧ Activities Director

Time was running out. I had to make a decision by the end of January about whether to register The Bigs for baseball that spring. They both wanted to play, but the thing is, I already registered them for soccer, which they also both wanted to play.

Not that I think it would be a bad thing to have these kids playing two sports. They would be five and seven in the spring. Young boys need all the exercise they can get. Mommies of young boys need them to get all the exercise they can get.

I was talking about this with our bowling league coordinator. We did the "when-we-were-kids" thing about how years ago we'd spend all day outside playing with our friends and didn't come in 'til the street lights came on. My, how times have changed. Whether it's because the world really has changed, or we've all increased our awareness of the boogeyman, kids just don't do that anymore.

I can barely get my kids to go out into our private, fenced-in backyard by themselves.

I recalled one unseasonably warm, sunny weekend day when The Bigs were overly energetic. My youngest was having a nap, and I would've liked one, too, since I'd had a grand total of five hours of sleep the night before. I had a wicked headache.

All I wanted the boys to do was go outside. We'd had enough indoor togetherness to last a very long time, kicked off by the "snow day" two Fridays prior when it rained all day.

And there we were, a couple of weeks later: after a spell of single-digit temps, it was finally in the forties. The boys were rowdy and silly, chock full of pent up energy.

"Take your light sabers *outside* boys! You're not going to get many more days like this during the winter. Here are your shoes — please don't step outside in those clean socks." I told them as I ushered them out the door.

Fifteen minutes later, they raced in, jockeying for position to be the first to present his side of their argument, tracking mud all the way to the couch where I'd collapsed.

"He hit me with his light saber!"
"Only because he hit me first!"

What I thought was: "Gee, boys, if you're going to be swinging light sabers at each other, someone's going to get hit, right?"
What I said was: "Why don't you find something else to do."

"Like what?" They both demanded.

I ticked off a list of suggestions including playing on the swing set, hitting baseballs, or picking up toys from the side yard.

"That's boring!"
"We can't — we hit all our balls over the fence!"
"I don't want to!"

Escorting them out the door again resulted in a ten-minute hiatus, before they came stomping back in, again tracking mud all over the foyer but this time leaving their boots, coats, and accessories shrugged off in a pile on the kitchen floor.

"I need a drink."
"I have to go to the bathroom."
"Okay, why don't you both get a drink and go to the bathroom."
"I don't need…"
"Do it anyway," I said.

Five minutes later they were back at the door.

"I forgot my Game Boy."
"You are not taking your Game Boy outside. It's a beautiful day!" I stood at the door, blocking their entry.
"But there's nothing to do!"
"The point of being outside is to get some exercise — run around the yard. Play catch. Bye bye." I closed the door.

They trudged back out reluctantly. In no time they were laughing like hyenas and throwing chunks of melting ice at our car and at the house. Before they started throwing it at passing traffic, I stalked out the door and said, "Go. Into the backyard. Where I can see you from the kitchen window."

"Can we go to the neighbor's house? She has a trampoline!"
"No. Backyard. Swing set."
"You're so mean…!"
"You never let us…!"

"Look boys, if you can't think of something constructive to do outside, you can come in and do chores."

They turned around. Fast.

I went back in and leaned on the door momentarily and sighed as I recalled how I used to dread the moment when the street lights flickered on.

My kids really needed to spend more time outside. It would be a good idea for these kids to play both sports. However, at ages five and seven, they wouldn't be on the same teams, as was the case with soccer the previous fall.

I remembered traipsing to two sets of practices and games every week, usually with their one-year-old brother in tow. Instead of sitting on the sidelines cheering, I'd spent most of my time herding my youngest off the field, while trying to keep whichever of the older two who wasn't playing in the game in my sight as he disappeared into the nether regions of the enormous complex of fields.

I realized that doubling the sports would complicate things exponentially. And given that I hadn't even factored in any ad hoc church, school, and scouting activities, I knew adding baseball wouldn't even be humanly possible.

I decided we'd skip baseball that spring.

❧ An Apple a Day

"Hand me a couple of curved pieces, would you, honey?" I asked him. My five-year-old and I were building a train track together on the floor of the room he shares with his big brother.

Nothing.

I looked up and saw him watching me, pensively.

He said, "So-and-so says 'your mom doesn't pack healthy lunches.'"

"Oh, is that so?" hackles rising immediately; this is kind of a sore subject.

"Yeah…"

"Well, what does *he* bring for lunch?" feeling inadequate, imagining all of the culinary delights that So-and-so's mommy serves up.

"Fruit."

"Oh. Well. What would you do if I put fruit in your lunch box?"

"Bleahhhhhh!" with an exaggerated hands-to-throat gagging gesture.

"Right. So that's why I don't do it."

He smiled at me and handed me the two curved pieces of track, as if that made all the sense in the world.

And it does to me — I have more control over plate waste if it happens at home.

"He doesn't see what you eat the rest of the time." No doubt he wouldn't be impressed, but was I really worried about what some other five-year-old thought about my son's lunch?

I continued, "It's really hard for me to make lunch for you, honey. You're very…uhm…selective."

In fact, getting that kid to eat anything other than cereal with milk these days is one of my biggest challenges.

I don't know how he became so hard to please! As a baby, he consumed anything I offered him — with great gusto. I have pictures of him eating berries we'd picked on the rail trail, raisins, peas, and pasta with red sauce — all things he won't touch today. There was one of him drinking a breakfast shake with a "Got Milk?" grin on his face. The pièce de résistance was a photo of him at six months old, gnawing on a beef rib bone. "Who's that baby!?" he wondered, as we looked through the photos together.

It's not that he hasn't been exposed to the things most other kids eat. I've insulted him with hamburgers, hot dogs, macaroni and cheese, SpaghettiO's®, several kinds of sandwiches — all of which repelled him, as garlic would a vampire. He insists he's allergic to peanut butter, which he is not, and survived on jelly sandwiches on white bread at camp all summer last year.

Currently his dietary staples — besides cereal and a limited sampling of other breakfast foods — include one or two kinds of pizza: Mystic and "mini-Mystic" (which is really just store-brand pizza made more desirable by my made up moniker), chicken nuggets, and fish sticks. He only recently resumed eating potato products. The choice du jour is shoestring fries, which is at least a delivery method for ketchup. While definitely not a vegetable, ketchup is at least good source of the anti-oxidant lycopene.

Then, and only because I won't allow "treat" unless he has fulfilled this requirement — he eats…drum roll, please…an apple. After all, an apple a day keeps the doctor away!

(And yes, I am aware that the experts say it's not a good idea to bribe children with food. Those experts have an open invitation to dinner at my house.)

❧ Kindergarten Registration

The sign stretched across Main Street announcing kindergarten registration made me cringe in remembrance of the year that I forgot to register my middle son for kindergarten.

When I realized my gaffe, I was one-and-a-half hours into a marathon business meeting. My cell phone didn't actually ring — because for once I had remembered to turn off all sounds — but it did everything it possibly could to make itself noticed from its position on the conference table (and I was not the only one who noticed it).

I looked at the number as I swiped the phone off the table and into my lap. It was a school number, but I couldn't answer it because I was sitting on the far side of the room with no easy escape.

"Tick tick tick" I thought impatiently. The presenter showed no signs of slowing down, even though it was half past the hour when I had expected they'd bring in lunch. Somewhat angst-ridden, I told myself if the caller left a voicemail, I'd listen to it right away, no matter what else was going on in that meeting.

Sure enough, the phone did its "notice me" routine again when the voicemail was delivered. It was my oldest's teacher telling me, "Nothing is wrong, I just wanted to call your attention to the kindergarten registration packet I'm sending home with your son…the deadline was today…"

"Oh, no…" I thought. I already had a registration packet at home. I felt like I'd been particularly clever to pick it up when I was visiting for my parent-teacher conference. I had also felt particularly triumphant that I'd actually shown up in person for this one, unlike the previous appointment, which wound up occurring over the phone, me sniffling as I stifled my tears, thinking what a loser parent I was to have spaced on my oldest son's first ever parent-teacher conference — even though I'd seen it in my calendar just the evening before.

It was a busy month (I was in sales at that time) and I had moved the registration packet from the kitchen counter to my desk to the dining room table, and to the end table in the living room, and every time I leafed through it, nothing compelled me to actually fill it out.

As soon as I could, I bolted for the door and called the school, ignoring the lunch that had finally arrived. As I scheduled the requisite screening appointment, I promised to have the paper work filled out and returned by the following Monday.

While the calendaring software I used for work was functional and up-to-date, I knew I was living on the edge in my personal day planner, where I entered (or forgot to enter) all of our family appointments.

Thankfully, today I no longer have to commute two-plus hours a day because I work full time in my home office. So while my personal day planner might be bulging with sticky notes and appointment cards and never seems to contain a pen, my work-life balance is pretty good.

Additionally, it'll be several years before I need to think about kinder-garten registration again.

✢ Going to Church Come Hell or High Water

One Sunday, as I tossed out three unused pledge envelopes before I got to the one with the current date, I was confronted with the fact that it had been four weeks since we'd been to church.

There had been reasons for our absences; in fact there were plenty of good excuses, but if I made them every week, missing church would be the rule rather than the exception.

The night before, I began promoting the idea, reminding the boys that it was "Church Day" tomorrow.

"NO MOMmmmeeeeee!" my oldest whined. "I don't wanna go!"

"Yeah, it's bow-wing!" his brother underscored.

The boys were particularly wild and rowdy that Sunday morning, yet I couldn't send them outside because it was raining. I stuck to my guns, though.

"Which of your *church* shirts do you want to wear today, boys?" I held up an assortment of clothes.

Fortunately, my youngest, who had awakened at 5:00 a.m., decided he needed a morning nap, so I popped in a *Bible Man* video for the The Bigs and seized the opportunity for a quick shower.

"Boys, are you dressed?" I called.

I heard giggling and rustling. Pajamas, pillows, and throws were flying as I walked through the living room and into the kitchen to assemble all the various and sundry items we'd need for a visit to church — diaper bag, quiet entertainment (books and toys that don't click, beep, or make truck noises), and snacks.

"Did you brush, boys, or are you going to church with pirate teeth today?"

I let my youngest sleep longer than I should have; I don't like breaking the "never wake a sleeping baby" rule. He clung to me as I rallied his reluctant brothers.

I herded them out the door, tossing their shoes out on the porch after them, and realized that the youngest had gone foo-foo. The break in the action while I changed his diaper triggered the The Bigs to resume bouncing off the walls and each other.

"Boys, just go wait outside! Please!"

I realized my youngest needed a new outfit, too, so I shoved some clothes into the diaper bag. I hauled him and all the bags out to the car, leaving his poopy clothes in a heap in the floor, a relative speck compared to the debris in the rest of the downstairs.

"No! No! No! No puddles, boys!"

During our journey, the rain became torrential, which necessitated my focusing on driving rather than the The Bigs' thrashing in the wayback of the car. By the time we got to church, one of them was sniffling and holding his white shirt up to his bloody nose. His brother was shouting, "SORRYSORRYSORRY! SOR-REE!!" in that obnoxious way that little boys have of being remorseful.

Umbrella-less, we hustled through the rain and into the church fellowship hall. The religious education director stopped in her tracks when she saw us. "I remember those days!" She also has three children, older than mine, so I was not embarrassed. As we stood there — late, bloody, soaked, naked, and disheveled — I was just grateful we made it — through hell and high water.

✎ A Bedtime Story for Electronic Media Junkies

"You should check out the book table!" someone suggested at a church fair once.

"Oh, no, no, no…we already have more books than we know what to do with."

"You can *never* have too many books!" she said in the scornfully condescending tone reserved for only the most severe parenting faux pas.

"Well, we do," I sang with a forced smile, and ushered the kids in a different direction. I didn't bother to explain that in addition to two full bookcases in the boys' rooms, one in the downstairs hallway, and the preschool books in abeyance in plastic tubs, I have boxes and boxes of my childhood books stored in the attic because my older kids are not interested in "boring *old* books" (to which many of us would refer as "classics") and I don't yet trust my youngest not to color in them. So why I need more than the couple hundred children's books we have is beyond me.

And why my big kids aren't more into books is beyond me, too. I read in front of them; I leave books, magazines, and newspapers in noticeable places; we often have stories at the dinner table (where I have a captive audience — for five minutes or so, anyway).

"But Mah-ahhhhm! We wanna watch a show!"

I wonder if I could rig up a treadmill to the TV so the kids could generate the power to run it themselves.

If it's not the TV, it's a Game Boy. Little electronic toys (with volume control) are good for ensuring compliance in the car, but more often than not I could beat a drum next to the kids and they wouldn't be able to tear their eyes off Mario and Luigi. I have caught my oldest with his Game Boy under the covers after lights out, and have even heard the telltale blips and beeps coming from the bathroom.

When I went to the public library as a child, it was to check out books — not videos — and not to play computer games or go to the playground.

They didn't have videos, computers, or a playground at my library when I was a kid (but there were such things as airplanes, cars, and electricity, I assure my kids). Fortunately they do come home with books from their school library.

One night after bath, my five-year-old asked me, "Can we watch a show?"

"Let's read your library book instead." There has been more than one morning when "it's library day already?" and we're scurrying around looking for the unread book to return.

"Awwwww. Darn it!"

"Oh, c'mon, boys, let's have a look. Ten minutes."

"Oh…all right…"
"I'll set the timer!"

I did different voices for all the characters and kept up a good pace so they wouldn't simply be counting down the minutes. To their credit, once we got started, they were engaged — jockeying for position and interrupting each other or me to make a point…

…until the timer went off. I finished the last page in double time.

"The …"

"Mommy, can we watch a show *now!?*"

"…end."

❧ My Heroes

One Monday morning, I was congratulating myself and my boys for getting out the door on time. They and all their accessories were in the car and the recycling was out for pick up. All I needed to do was roll the big trashcan from the side yard to the street and we'd be on our way.

But, I froze in my tracks. On top of the gate that leads to our enclosed side yard was a dead baby bird.

I cringed and shuddered and couldn't bring myself to open the gate. "Oh no!" I said.

"What's wrong, Mommy?" one of my sons called out his car window.

"Dead bird…" I grimaced, one hand at my throat, the other pointing. Earlier in the month, we had discovered and begun watching the nest in the wisteria bush that grew on the tall fence separating our driveway and side yard.

"Where?"

"Let me see!"

My older two scrambled out of the car.

"Would you guys hold the gate open, please, while I get the trash can out?"

"Sure, Mommy."

Then, I noticed that there were some bird body parts on the ground. The night before we'd experienced a torrential rainstorm. It must have washed all the baby birds out of the nest, which was eerily silent and looked empty. I saw the displaced Mommy bird sitting in the neighbor's tree. My stomach was in knots.

I paced as I texted my neighbor: "Dead bird on gate. I can't deal. Please move it? TYVM." Then I moved the trash can.

When I returned from the curb, my boys were standing on a little table getting a closer look.

Trying not to gag, I began brushing the bird body parts under the hosta plants next to the porch with a fallen branch. Moments later, my middle son was cradling the dead bird in his hands reverently, his older brother by his side. "Wanna see, Mommy?"

"No, honey!" I shrank away and covered my eyes. "Bushes," I said, pointing in the general direction of the corner of our back yard.

"C'mon, Mom, just take a look."

"I can't!" I said, emphatically. "But I'll take your picture." I pulled out my cell phone, which includes a camera. I sent my neighbor the picture with "Never mind."

Normally I'm not so squeamish: I don't want to predispose my boys to any opinions about bugs, spiders, worms, or creepy crawlies, which I embrace with feigned abandon whenever they are presented to me. I try to teach them to respect all God's creatures.

My son carried the bird gingerly as he walked along the stone path in our garden, stopping at the bushy spot next to the big tree where ivy abounds.

"Rest in peace, little bird," he said, setting it down gently.

My eyes filled with tears.

"Mommy, what's wrong?"

"Oh, nothing really, boys…it's all part of the circle of life, right?"

It was gratitude that had choked me up then — because, while the storm had knocked out our electricity for nearly five hours the night before, we had been safe and sound in our "nest."

❧ At Your Service

"Mom, can you get me _____ <fill in with "my homework," "a drink," "my Game Boy," or "a pair of socks.">

"Not right now, honey, _____ <fill in the blank with "I'm doing the dishes," "my hands are full," "but maybe after I change this diaper," or "I've got the baby in the bathtub.">

"But Mah-am! You're closer."
"Yes, but, I'm *busy*. You're perfectly capable…and anyway, I'm not your servant…"

"You never do anything for us!"

What is so absurd about that comment is that everything I do is for them or because of them.

My children are my "why." They are why I get up in the morning (usually earlier than I would like to), why I go to work every day, why I "vacation" at a local beach rather than at a Caribbean resort, why I drive a Mommy-wagon, why I have toast crusts for breakfast and half-eaten chicken "noggins" for dinner, why eating out and going to the theater means having dinner on the porch (because the dining room table is covered with laundry and homework papers) and seeing animated films at the movie theater (rather than borrowing them from the library), why our house is decorated in the fingerprint-and-strewn-toy motif, and so on ad infinitum.

I really *am* their servant. I spend most of the time when they are awake at home serving them in some way. I am a cook, waiter, janitor, nurse-maid, laundress, chauffer, referee, tutor, spiritual advisor, activities director, drill sergeant, and will step into myriad other roles on an ad hoc, on-demand basis.

I've known from the moment they were born, that my job and my joy has been to nurture them along until they can become self-sufficient. I must remain committed to my mission even though it's bittersweet to observe how sophisticated my two school-aged sons have become compared to the innocent exuberance of their two-year-old brother.

A Salary.com study concludes that if paid the salary of the equivalent work a mother performs, a woman would earn between $85K and just over $138K, depending on whether she was a "working mother" or a stay-at-home mother. (Hello? Aren't all mothers working mothers? Surely, what they mean is "income-earning mothers.")

I don't get rewarded in dollars for my motherwork. Instead, my compensation is that my children are my motivation, my inspiration, and my revelation. It is because of my three little muses that I know the true love of God, which radiates through me to them and then reflects back. Proudly, I wear their boogers, drool, and other wipings on my shoulders like epaulettes. And while one day my servitude will end, no matter how independent they become, the emotional umbilical cord will remain unsevered.

❧ Dirty Dishes

"Dish soap, dish soap, dish soap," I chanted to keep myself on track. I was poking around the house, looking everywhere I'd gone since I'd returned from my early morning supermarket trip, squeezed in between daycare drop off and beginning work for the day in my home office.

That's my favorite time of day to go grocery shopping. It's incredibly peaceful compared to the experience I have when accompanied by my kids. "Can we get…?" "I want that…!" "But why can't we…!?" "You're so mean!" "I hate…!" "I have to go potty *now!*"

I can barely get a word in edgewise: "No." "No!" "Because you already had…!" "Put that back, please." "Watch out for that display…uh, oh… whoa!" "Why didn't you tell me sooner?"

It was lunchtime and I wanted to fix something to eat but had to clear the decks first. I'd forgotten to buy dish soap when I went shopping earlier in the week, and had watered down the last quarter inch of my existing soap too many times already.

Sure, I could probably re-organize the mess in the sink in order to avoid actually washing the dishes (and yes, we do have a dishwasher but I don't use it regularly since we usually run out of silverware before it's ready to run). However, this was a matter of principle. I really wanted that new soap, which was the catalyst for the other $70 worth of other stuff I'd picked up. Funny how that had happened when it had only been four days since I'd been shopping…

I couldn't find it anywhere.

While I was microwaving some leftover soup, I burrowed through my purse for the grocery store receipt to confirm that I had actually purchased the soap.

I called the supermarket. "Uhhhm. Hi. I think I left a bag in my cart this morning. It's not here, anyway…"

"What was in it?" the woman at the courtesy booth asked, courteously.

"Dish soap. Oh, and probably baby wipes, too…"

"Yes. I have it…I'll keep it for you right here."

"Great, thanks. I'll be by later on," I said, as I rinsed off a spoon and began eating my lunch out of its plastic container.

But as the day wore on, I knew I wasn't going to make it into the store anytime soon. I had back-to-back conference calls and when I met the school bus I had my headset on. At 5:00 we needed to go to pick up my youngest at daycare, which is right across the street from the supermarket. Should we rush into the supermarket before (two kids, one extra left turn on a busy road with no stoplights during commuter hour, and the risk of being late for pick up with a $1.00 per minute penalty) or go after when we weren't in such a hurry (three kids, two extra left turns, with the risk of a cranky toddler who doesn't understand why his normal routine is disrupted)?

Neither scenario was all that desirable.

That night we dined on paper plates.

✎ Haute Wheels

"Wow, nice ride!" a dad-friend said to me in the church parking lot one Sunday.

I never imagined that having a station wagon would be "cool." The closest thing I had to cool was a two-door sports car with T-tops — that was more than 15 years prior, before I moved on to sensible and professional four-door sedans.

When my first two children came along, I lamented not having a minivan, not only because it would be really useful, but also (as I imagined) because it was a membership prerequisite for "Club Mom." Sometimes I felt like I just didn't measure up. (Actually, in all honesty, even though I'm over my van envy, I still feel that way occasionally.)

Before my youngest was born, I considered the van idea again. However, I was commuting two-plus hours a day at that time and didn't think a van was practical. So I simply got a larger sedan that would fit three car seats across the back. It was an older car with a powerful automatic transmission, a bit on the buoyant side.

It wasn't long before I realized that having three little boys across the backseat was somewhat of a nightmare. The youngest had to be in the middle so I could reach out and touch him. But that meant he was right in the line of fire between the older two, who could also reach out and touch him. Whichever of the The Bigs sat behind me would kick my seat incessantly. I knew it was not always on purpose — booster seats don't have leg rests, so how comfortable can they really be — but that wasn't top of mind every time I felt those little feet pummeling my back.

I endured this for eighteen months while imagining how to implement some sort of separation between front and back à la limousines, taxi cabs, and police cars, before I had to face the fact: it was time to revisit the seven-passenger vehicle plan.

After much consideration, I chose a "practical and safe" (according to an automotive.com review) station wagon with a rear-facing third-row bench seat. Though someone else had depreciated the car for more than five years for me and it now features the same interior design theme as our home (toys, books, crumbs), it's still the nicest car I've ever had.

There are more bells and whistles than I currently need, such as a built-in programmable garage door opener (we don't have a garage); cruise control (not really necessary on our main road, even though it *is* a numbered route); and sound system controls on the steering wheel (I don't feel that the center console is too far to reach).

I looked at my church friend quizzically for a moment *"Could he be serious?"* He didn't even know about the car's "sporty suspension tuning and the five-speed manual transmission" on my "high-output turbo T5 model that makes the car fun to drive" (also from the online review).

I simply answered, "Thanks — we like it!"

I must be dwelling in a parallel universe — to the one in which I existed pre-children — if a Carol-Brady car is "haute."

❧ The Annual Visit

This year my son's annual physical was even more excruciating than mine.

Mixed in with the questions about guns (no), cigarette smoking (no), smoke and carbon monoxide detectors (yes), we faced the following three biggies:

1) "Where do you sleep at night?

"With my brother. In my bedroom. Sometimes in Mommy's bed. Sometimes Mommy sleeps in our room…"

Raised eyebrows. "You all sleep in the same room?" Turning to me, "Does he sleep through the night in his own bed?"

"Well, he starts out there…"

The nurse made some notes on my son's chart.

2) "How much TV do you watch?"

My son looked blankly and unblinkingly at the nurse, akin to the way he stares at the tube.

The nurse redirected his question to me, "How many hours a day is the TV on?"

"Uhmmmm"…while I tried to calculate, I wondered if this meant TV as in cable, or did that count videos and DVDs, too…and what about other electronic media like the Game Boy?…Hmmmmm…"Probably two or three hours."

My estimate was likely on the shy side, and yet it still sounded like a lot. I wondered if the nurse even believed me, or if he would add time to that, the same way my doctor would likely add pounds to my estimate of my weight, if the scale didn't tell the naked truth (because I usually like to get as naked as possible before getting weighed, which is unfortunate when the scale is in the hallway outside the doctor's office).

"I see." Pause. Scribble.

Right about when I was beginning to question our family lifestyle and my parenting choices, came the pièce de résistance…

3) "Do you eat all the food groups?"

"I like the dessert food group the best! Cackle, snort!"

The food pyramid had been a Cub Scout activity this past year, with all the kids cutting pictures of food out of supermarket fliers to glue onto a chart for presentation at their pack meeting. The "sweets category" was a tiny triangle at the top of the pyramid, but it was so heavily populated with pictures of cake and brownie mix, ice cream, soda, boxed cookies and donuts, and candy that there was barely room for anything else on the posterboard.

"How's his diet?" The nurse apparently gave up on getting a serious answer from my son.

"Well, that's about the gist of it. He does eat cheese, yogurt, chicken "noggins," fish sticks, some other kid-food like hot dogs and Spaghetti-O's®, all manner of potato products…he doesn't really eat too many vegetables… oh, well, carrots count, right?…but he does eat an apple just about every day and likes some other fruits, too…" I rambled.

Was it getting warm in there?

The nurse made one final notation and snapped the folder closed. "The doctor will be right in."

Moments later, the doctor arrived, poring over my son's chart as he walked through the door. "Do you have any concerns about your son's vision or hearing?"

"No, not really…only his listening…" I replied in an effort to add some levity to the situation, while simultaneously praying for an expeditious end to the visit.

❧ Play Therapy

I was in the middle of an insanely busy period at work, gearing up for a conference where more than 6000 of my company's customers and business partners would "come together to reset the pace for innovation." There would be world-renowned keynotes! World-famous entertainment! And world-class education value! All in the fabulous city of Las Vegas! One of my colleagues and I were preparing to run a booth and were politicking to find opportunities to promote it within corporate confines.

"That ought to be a fun getaway," one of my well-meaning friends offered, when I lamented that I still needed to make travel plans, order new business cards, and tie up some childcare loose ends.

"This isn't a vacation — I'll be working the whole time and probably won't ever leave the hotel. And my regular work isn't gonna go away…" I huffed, feeling Dilbertesque.

In fact, there was still so much to do before I could even embark on my Las Vegas extravaganza, I wound up working late most evenings. One night, as I scanned the next day's jam-packed calendar, I saw that I had "Reading in Ms. So-and-so's class." I was at the point where I was cutting bait on all things non-essential to the conference. But there was no way I could cut that.

I was due in the classroom at 12:30. I had blocked my calendar 15 minutes early so I could walk to school. *At least I'll get some exercise.* But no — I crammed one more to-do into my morning and wound up driving the half mile to school, sprinting to the office to sign in, and race-walking to the classroom since "there's no running in the halls."

Crossing the classroom threshold, I stepped into chaos of another sort — happy, hopeful, exuberance. My middle son's face lit up when we locked eyes, and I shrugged off my corporate cloak. My role was to sit with and moderate the kids on the floor, listen to Ms. So-and-so while she read a book, and then facilitate a game with groups of four to six kids, as they rotated through several different reading-related activities.

I have always been amazed and inspired by Ms. So-and-so's patience. She was my oldest son's teacher the year before and I have never seen her lose her cool or be judgmental. She has the equanimity of our GPS receiver, Lucy. We don't like to drive without Lucy: If we make a wrong turn she doesn't say anything — she simply re-routes us and never lets on that we have made a mistake. She is so understanding. She also displays the answer to the mercifully unasked question, "When are we gonna get there?"

It was all I could do to manage the game and the children. Their concerns about how to spell four-letter words were interspersed with who was their best friend that day, what was for hot lunch, and whether they might have indoor or outdoor recess. There were no hidden agendas and it was easy to forgive their tactlessness. My job was momentarily irrelevant.

I left the classroom that day channeling Ms. So-and-so's patience and political-correctness, as I prepared to embrace the opportunity for a business trip.

After all, I'd be able to eat grown up food, socialize with other adults (some of them colleagues that I had worked with for years but never met face-to-face), and enjoy some world-famous entertainment — all in the fabulous city of Las Vegas!

❧ Schtick and Tired: Comic Themes Related to Sleeping — Or Not

In the morning, on a school day

"Rise and shine boys, it's already 6:30!"
"Is it a school day?"
"Yes! Time to get up, get going, get your spirit showing!" (I was a cheer-leader at one time in my life).
"If it's a school day, I'm still tired!"

In the morning, on a weekend

"Mommy." Poke, poke, nudge. "It's time to get up!"
"No, it isn't honey," I whisper. "We're all still sleeping."
Urgently: "Mommy! It's five-four-four."
"That's okay, honey. It's Sunday. We don't have to go anywhere until church."
Silence. Then, "But I *want* to get up."
"Shhhh."
"Mom-mee-ee-ee!" he nudges me again.
"Get up then. Go ahead, honey."
"But I want you to come with me!"

In the afternoon, any day

From the second-floor bedroom: "Mah-ahm…"

"Oh, dear God. *Why* isn't that kid asleep?" I dread the idea that he won't nap, because that means he'll be really cranky in the evening. Or else, he'll have a late nap, be cranky when I wake him up for dinner, be up too late (making me cranky), and thus be cranky the next morning.

"Mommy?" he calls again tentatively.
I consider ignoring him, praying that he'll give up, roll over, and snooze.

"Mommy!"
"Mama!"
I consider too long.

"MOMMEEEEE!"
"MA! MAAAAAAH!!!"
He's increasingly impatient that I have not yet arrived.

"What is it, honey? You can't be yelling like that! What is it!?" I ask, somewhere between a whisper and a hiss, so as not to wake the sleeping
brother in the next bed.

"I'm hungry. No, I'm thirsty. No, I'm…"
Right. He's probably just tired.

At night, on a weekend

"Can we stay up as late as we want?"
"Sure, boys! Why don't you see if you can stay up until midnight?"
"Awright! Thanks, Mom!"
Both are asleep before 8:30.

At night, on a weeknight

"Boys, time for bed."
"Awwww. Ten more minutes?"
"No, it'll be ten minutes by the time you're ready for bed."
"But we're not tired."
"You still need to go potty and brush. So, let's go."
"We don't wanna!"
"Yeah, we're NOT going."
"Boys, if you don't go willingly, there will be a consequence. You know the
deal. It's the same every night. Get up off the couch. Go in the bathroom.
One of you go potty while the other brushes. Then switch."
"We can't."
"Why not?"
"We're too tired!"

Later, on a weeknight

Mommeeeeeeee! Calling from upstairs.
"What? What is it!?" Me running up quickly, thinking there's something
dire going on / not wanting the baby to wake up.
"Can you turn the light on more?"

"Mommeeeeeeee!" Repeat the drill three more times.
Insert: "I'm thirsty." "Can you cover me up?" "What are you doing down there?"

"That's it. You.Must.Go.To.Sleep.Now.Tomorrow.Is.A.School.Day. If I have to come up here again…"

The next morning, my son asks, "Is it a school day?"
"Yes! Time to get up, get going…"
"If it's a school day, I'm still tired!"

❧ To T or Not To T

"I don't wanna go!" my middle son said adamantly, his arms crossed. He was slouched as far down as the seatbelt would allow and his feet were pressing insistently against the back of my seat.

He'd asserted this fact repeatedly during the previous week, to which I'd deferred, "Well, let's see how you feel when the day comes." But the day had arrived and he'd refused to budge from his position. "I'm *not* gonna play!"

"Right.Well." *Ahem*. "That's up to you, but we owe your coach and your team the courtesy of showing up and you can tell them yourself."

We were in the car on the way to his first T-ball practice. The whole after-noon had been scheduled around his first T-ball practice. I had to pick my youngest up from daycare early, which had cut way into my work day. I telecommute, so I knew I could make up the time later, but that often meant working a lengthy "third shift," (the first being the regular workday, which often overlapped with the second, which was family time). I'd heated up chicken "noggins" and smiley fries so we could tailgate. An-noyed, I added, "And stop kicking my seat."

Indeed, our whole spring had been scheduled around T-ball. We had skipped the previous year (though he'd had a season of T-ball when he was going on four), because he and his older brother were already on dif-ferent teams for spring soccer. They are just a grade apart in school, but nearly 17 months apart in age, and while every other season or so they can be on the same team, the previous spring the age cutoff didn't work out. I couldn't imagine two teams per kid so we took a pass on baseball.

However, we never skipped playing catch in the back yard, and my middle son, at age five was good — at least as good as his seven-year-old brother. That year, I had to go out and buy myself a softball glove because I could no longer catch barehanded. They could both hit the ball without a T: our neighbors were constantly tossing initialed balls back over our fence.

My middle son especially had been so disappointed at being sidelined, he reminded me frequently between June and January when registration for the following spring began. Since the boys were slated to be on the same soccer team, I went ahead and signed them both up for baseball, as well. I knew that with some modification to our schedule and carpooling assistance, I'd be able to pull it off.

I was blindsided by his change of heart.

We arrived at the field on time, but my son refused to get out of the car. "I'm not gonna get out!"

I ignored him. I got the compliant brothers situated on a spectator bench with their dinner and then went back to the car. I insisted he out and join us *right now*.

He refused.

I persisted. "Take the first step, *just get out!*"

Reluctantly he did. Scowling, he slumped against the fence that divided the parking lot from the field, plucking at blades of grass.

Woop-woop. Aiming the remote over my shoulder, I locked the car as I stalked back to his brothers on the bench.

I smiled through clenched teeth as I waved at the coach, signed something on the clipboard that was passed around, and accepted a copy of the snack-and-treat schedule that another very proactive mom had already prepared and continued to act as if nothing was wrong.

The kids had paired up to play catch. My oldest, whose help I had enlisted to "please set a good example, I'm counting on you" stood in for his brother, even though he was far too cool for T-ball, since he was now in the "coach-pitch" league. The coach handed him a team hat.

My middle son approached our bench a few times, snagging chicken and fries each time.

First he asked for his Nintendo DS (his hand-held dual-screen video game console). "There's nothing to do!"

"What do you mean there's nothing to do — we're at baseball practice!"

"I'm tired!"

"I'm sure if you got up and ran around with the other kids you'd feel energized."

"Mah-ahm," he whined, "I just don't feel so good…"

I disregarded that last comment, but began to waver in my conviction. *The kid is only six. Should I force him to honor his original commitment? If I let him bail out before he even got started, would he always be a quitter? Would he ever play baseball again? Would it be one of those things he'd regret forever? Was I being dramatic? The kid is not quite six…*

I noticed with the eyes in the back of my head that my son had moved closer to the spectator bench. I continued to pay no attention to him and instructed his little brother to do the same.

Soon it was time for the coach to start a batting and fielding drill. My oldest continued to sub for his brother and was a pretty good sport, given that this was T-ball, after all, and there were boys and even dumb-old-yucky girls on the team. Some kids were so "babysish" (at age five) and — unable to discern all the chaos of their coach, parent volunteers, and teammates yelling, "Run, run, run!" "Go back!" — would realize they were stacked up two on a base with another one coming when they peered out from under their batting helmets. Those of us on the spectator benches cheered and clapped and laughed.

"Geez, don't they know anything?" my middle son asked, scornfully. He was standing right behind me.

"Maybe not, honey. For some of these kids it might be their first time ever."

Finally, 45 minutes into the practice, he inserted himself into the batting line up next to his older brother and took the "Cardinals" hat off his brother's head. My oldest sat with his brother until it was time for him to bat, then rejoined us on our bench.

At the end of the practice, the coach handed out the team jerseys and the very proactive mom handed out popsicles. My son charged over, "Look what number I got, Mom!" as he threw popsicles at his brothers.

With almost every fiber of my being, I wanted to deliver the "I-told-you-so" lecture. Instead, I bit my tongue and conjured up, "Oh, that's great, honey! That means you'll bat right after so-and-so!"

✤ Happiness Must Be Grown in One's Own Garden

In the time I have lived in the house that I do, there's often been someone else around to take care of the yard and garden, but currently, most of this responsibility lies with me. This has always been one of the chores I've eschewed, not only because someone else did it, but because I figured "I'm too busy with what's going on inside the house," e.g., my three children and my job, which I do at home.

However, one year, I realized that I could no longer put off the inevitable Spring cleanup when a friend pointed out that raking up "all those leaves" (that I had ignored not only in the warmer months but also as far back as the previous Autumn) might be a good service project for our church youth group. Initially my excitement about getting that project done overshadowed my embarrassment that she'd noticed what a mess my yard was.

But then I realized that it wouldn't be fair to expect someone else to do something I'm perfectly capable of doing. I figured the youth group should spend their time helping someone who really needed it: my older two children have reached the age where they do not need constant supervision outside, and they can actually assist in managing their younger brother. This means we can all be outside together and I can do something other than herd them away from the front yard (which is only a small strip of grass between our home and a busy street) or push them in the swings. Besides, it would be a good opportunity to teach them about yard work.

So I committed to tackling the project. The following Monday I got out the rake.

Over the course of the next month — a little at a time — I managed to clean up most of the leaves (though I decided to let the ones that are now mostly hidden behind the day lilies rest in peace), plant some seeds, and pull out weeds.

The boys and I went to a garden store to pick out some flowers and when the guy ringing us up did a double take at the eclectic mix we'd chosen (anything blue for my oldest, anything red for my middle, and anything goes for the youngest), and my insistence that we needed not one, but three, "boy-colored" watering cans, I told him, "I'm not just growing flowers, I'm growing children."

The boys have done a little weeding and watering, which has mostly consisted of flooding the flower beds, making a mud puddle at the bottom of the slide that's part of our swing set, soaking each other, or whacking dandelions with baseball bats. I've been digging dandelions out of the front yard (to keep up with the proverbial "Joneses"), but I am not militant about this — especially in the back yard — since I appreciate receiving the little yellow bouquets thrust at me with small fists. I also like making dandelion seed wishes just as much as the boys do, something that makes many a lawn aficionado cringe.

One day my neighbor across the street came over and relieved me of my lawn-mowing duties. He also helped me figure out what was a weed and what was not, validating my opinion that if I like it, it can stay (including the violets that punctuate the lawn alongside the remaining dandelions). This means that my gardens are a random mix of flowers, ivy and other ground cover, some sort of bush with prickly tentacles, something else that looks like it's part of the onion family, as well as some bare spots, where the seeds we planted were likely washed away by overzealous watering. (I'll probably put perennial bulbs there when I figure out when is the right time to plant them). I rearranged the lawn statues, sundial, and birdbath (that my mom left behind when she moved across the country) to suit my own taste.

One time as I was unrolling the hose, I surveyed my little quarter acre plot of the American dream, and was reminded of a sentiment that graces one of my sets of greetings cards: "Happiness must be grown in one's own garden." I realized that my garden is a visual representation of my life: it is lush and colorful and welcoming to friends and family; at the same time, there are thorny parts, non-conforming parts, and empty parts, as well as some bugs. It's not perfect by any means, but there's a tremendous amount of beauty and joy, even in unlikely places. It's a work in progress and I'm responsible for it.

And then I stuck my thumb over the end of the hose to spray water gently into the birdbath, and made my own rainbow.

❧ Don't Leave Home Without It

Summer camp had ended and it was time to start thinking about going back to school. Aside from still needing to process the paperwork that I'd set aside in June, I decided I'd clean out the backpacks the boys had been lugging to camp every day.

They were obviously carrying some excess baggage: they reminded me of turtles sometimes as they shuffled out to the car, trying to squeeze through the porch door simultaneously. I wondered if one of them tipped over and landed on his back, could he get up?

Typical morning exchanges in our house included the following:

"Where's my DS?"
"I'm not in charge of your DS, honey."

"I can't get my towel in here!"
"Maybe if you took out some of the other stuff you don't really need…?"

"Mommy, can you carry this? It's way too heavy!" (whine)
"Absolutely not — it's *your* backpack."

I decided to launder the backpacks in addition to simply emptying them. I dumped their contents on top of the dryer.

Backpack one included
• Home made paper money in denominations ranging from one to ten trillion dollars with a few $297s and other unusual amounts in the mix
• Seven screw-on bottle caps
• Five toy cars
• Two blobs of dried up play dough substance
• A plastic 50-cent piece
• A "lost" Power Ranger action figure
• A dead bee in a small plastic container
• One large rock

Backpack two contained
• A dead grasshopper in a small plastic container
• Five paper airplanes

- A scrap of paper with a tic tac toe game on it
- Three crunched up bookmarks
- A folded piece of paper with cut out shapes
- A squished piece of unchewed gum, mostly liberated from its wrapper with sand and leaves stuck to it
- Two Beyblade tops, all accessories included
- Empty Yu-Gi-Oh! card holder
- Cootie catcher
- Plastic New England Patriots logo tag
- Feather
- Assorted plastic piñata trinkets
- Two Star Wars figurines
- A toy car
- Green plastic cockroach
- Birthday party blower
- Nintendo DS
- 13 plastic monkeys

This was not even including the stuff that fell off the dryer and went wherever the missing socks go.

"What a couple of packrats!" I tsk-ed to myself. Then realized how frequently I resorted to dumping the contents of my purse out in an effort to get to my phone before it stopped ringing. I decided I'd take stock of my own baggage while the washing machine ran.

I was chagrined to find far too many items that either belonged in the trash (expired coupons, old receipts, five pieces of a broken pen, and orange-colored crumbs), or that I didn't even need on a regular basis (MBTA passes, a luggage key that probably went to the carry-on briefcase I had last locked in early 2005 and yes, even a pair of winter gloves).

Knowing that the size of the bag determines the amount of stuff one carries around, I scoured my closet to find something more fashionable, i.e., smaller, to replace the diaper-bag sized purse I'd been toting.

And I couldn't help but wonder how long it will be before our bags runneth over again…

❧ Dress-code Double Standard

"You're *still* wearing your pajamas?" My oldest son said to me as he and his brother got off the school bus.

"No, honey, of course not! This is 'lounge wear'!" I answered, maybe a little defensively. I wondered if my elementary school-aged sons were already embarrassed of their mom in front of their friends on the bus.

"They *look* like pajamas to me…"

Technically, he's right. I think "lounge wear" is just the dressed-up name for pajamas. And even if I didn't have said lounge wear on, I'd be wearing some sort of pajama-level-of-comfort clothes, i.e., yoga pants and a hoodie. This is one of the primary benefits of working at home, contrary to popular belief that it is the savings in gas and wear and tear on the car.

I felt a little pang of guilt, because for the second year now, I'd imposed a back-to-school dress code on the older boys, but have no such standards in place for myself.

During the summer their drawers will overflow with t-shirts that have all manner of sports themes or cartoon characters. And due to their "LIFO" methodology of clothing inventory management — last-in, first-out — they tend to get into a rut: the same Power Rangers, Pokémon, and Disney characters shirts appear every few days. All the cute little "collar shirts" will be worn only once a week, if that — to church. Ensuring that the red Pikachu shirt or the black spiderweb shirt are clean and available on any given day is tiresome.

So, at the end of last summer, I removed all the t-shirts, and replaced them with eight or so collar shirts each, and thus began the differentiation between school shirts and play shirts (no one has yet pointed out that Mommy always wears play shirts).

I did not do the same with their pants — and their little chinos and jeans are slowly phasing out of their wardrobes. Both of my older boys favor "soft pants," which translates to athletic pants. They even like the ones that, when they walk, are reminiscent of crickets. How can I complain?

The boys bought in to the dress code, and for a long time wore their shirts buttoned all the way up to the top (which was eventually remedied by peer pressure), sometimes asking for an assist to get that last button done. When they began to miss their superheros or "The Mouse," and the getting-dressed-in-the-morning battles began, rather than start everyone's day with an explosive confrontation, we compromised with "casual Fridays."

I smoothed my oldest son's collar as I guided him across the street to our house (God forbid should I hug him in front of his friends). "Well, honey, I assure you, these are *not* pajamas."

❧ Here's Mud in Your Eye

I was up to my eyeballs in the "project from hell" — drinking too much coffee and biting my cuticles off because the only thing consistent or predictable about the project was that the scope of work would be changed on a regular basis.

On one particular day, there was a status meeting that had been rescheduled no fewer than three times. Ultimately it was set for 4:30, which would be iffy for me because this was one of the two days a week that I met my middle son at the school bus, and made up work time after the kids went to bed.

As fate would have it, that day I got a call from the school nurse about my middle son who'd been stomping in mud puddles at recess, got dirt in his eye, and must have scratched it because he could no longer open it.

Of all days, I thought, and told her I'd be there in ten minutes. I dashed over to the school and found my son wearing an eye patch. When he saw me with his good eye, he began to cry.

I picked him up like a baby, thanked the nurse, and carried all 60 pounds of him out. I secured a 3:45 doctor's appointment, even though I knew there was a risk that I'd either be late for my 4:30 meeting or have to call in from the road.

We were early for our appointment, but wound up waiting 20 minutes anyway. My son sat on my lap and buried his face in my neck and hair, feeling self conscious about the eye patch. When I finally carried him in to the doctor's office, nothing either of us did could convince, cajole, or coerce him to open his eye to let the doctor take a peek. The doctor said he'd have to refer us to a specialist. It was 4:15 at that point.

I wish I could say that I didn't give another thought to traipsing across town to the ophthalmologist's office, but that isn't the case. I thought first about the additional time it would take, and how was I ever going to make that project meeting?

I lugged my son out to the parking lot and situated him in the car. It was 4:30. I called the conference number, but no one was there. So I called one of my colleagues, who told me the meeting had been changed to

4:50, "didn't you see the reschedule notice?" I groaned inwardly (the notice could have only come in the last hour, since I'd been glued to my computer up until that point), and told her I'd talk with her later.

At the ophthalmologist's office, we were ushered right in to a cozy, warm, and dark room. As my son snuggled on my lap, I realized that *I* was the one who needed to get the proverbial mud out of my eye. It became clear to me that this time with my son could not be interrupted or deferred. There was no way I'd be available for any other meeting.

✎ Don't Dis the DS

"Aren't you afraid it will rot their brains?" My friend was observing my two older boys sitting in rapt attention on the couch, sharing a Nintendo® DS. This was the only thing my oldest had asked Santa for two years in a row (the first year Santa didn't think a DS was appropriate for a child his age). Neither of them had heard me ask if they wanted a snack.

"Not at all, I replied. "I think they can learn something from them."

"Oh, c'mon — don't try to tell me they play educational games on those things."

"Well, yes, in fact, we do have one called 'Brain Games'…" my answer trailed off, though, because in all honesty no one plays that one much. "… But lately they've been more into Star Wars, Mario Cart, and Metroid."

"I didn't think so," my friend said, smugly.

"Well, still, simply playing with electronic games helps kids develop critical thinking skills."

"Ha!" My friend scoffed.

"Hey — you can't escape technology…" I answered, lightheartedly. (I certainly can't — I work for one of the world's largest technology enterprises.)

"Right, right," my friend said, cutting me off, obviously not buying it.

I was sure my viewpoint wasn't simply skewed by corporate ethnocentrism: I have heard a lot lately about digital games-based learning.

Research shows the benefits of games in teaching skills children will need in a twenty-first-century economy, pointing to the military use of games to teach strategy, laproscopic surgeons who play games as a "warm-up" before surgery, and entrepreneurs who played games growing up. Kids can learn about problem solving, language and cognitive skills, strategic thinking, collaboration, prudent risk taking, strategy formulation and execution, as well as complex moral and ethical decisions.

I changed my approach with my friend. "Alright, then, if for no other reason, it's their currency. They have to meet certain requirements in order to have the privilege of playing it." (Sometimes the requirement was I simply needed them to be still and quiet, but I didn't mention that, because I didn't need the "electronic babysitter debate," either).

"It's a good way to ensure compliance," I said with finality. It wasn't worth discussing further with my friend, whose mind was already made up.

I called to my sons from the kitchen, "Boys — snack?"

No reply.

I walked over to the boys with a plate of muffins and inserted it between their eyes and the DS. They looked at the plate, looked at me blankly and then looked at the plate again before pausing their game.

Apparently their multitasking and parallel processing skills need further development.

❧ He Ain't Heavy, He's My Baby

One time, a bunch of my friends and our kids and I walked from my house down Main Street to a parade. I figured my youngest would scamper along with the rest of the kids, but no. He walked about half a block before he announced, "I wan carryou." So, I picked him up and carried him the five blocks or so.

We arrived at the parade origin and he continued to cling like a koala. He was sucking his thumb, people-watching, as we waited for the parade to start.

And then, "I wan my lowie," he said urgently, leaning over. He was referring lovey, which must have fallen to the ground when I shifted him onto my other hip.

"*Than* gyoo," he sang as I handed it to him. He laid it across my shoulder and put his head down.

The parade formed, and we marched alongside it until it ended at the town field. All the kids dashed up to the library playground, except for my youngest, who had fallen asleep. I found a bench and rocked him while kids and parents scurried about, checking in and chatting from time to time.

We all traipsed back to our house on the rail trail, me lagging behind, lugging my slumbering son. I hauled him straight up to bed, laid him down gently, and pulled off his shoes. But…

…*where was his lovey!?*

It wasn't on either of my shoulders. "Please let it be somewhere in the house," I prayed, thinking maybe I had dropped it in the foyer when I paused to kick off my shoes or somewhere en route to his upstairs room. It wasn't. Panic set in.

I told my friends I'd be right back and dashed out. Yes, we have more than one lovey, but my son knows the difference and sometimes favors his "notherwon lowie" or wants "one-two-three lowies." Besides, this was the blue one with his name on it.

I had no idea how long he would sleep, so I ran. Thoughts of him waking up without his lovey had renewed my strength. I got back on the trail and bolted all the way to the oil company a quarter of a mile down the path before I spotted it. Time stood still for a moment: I felt as though I was running in slow motion — as sometimes happens in dreams — with all the sentiment evoked by the theme song from *Chariots of Fire*.

Defying bike path etiquette, I made a beeline for it, cutting off a few cyclists who were obviously training for the next Tour de France. I know this because I had to pardon their French as they swerved and braked to avoid first me and then the lovey lying in their path.

I snatched up the lovey and clutched it to my chest, choking not only for breath but also on the lump in my throat. I racewalked back home. My son only stirred as I tucked the lovey in next to him. He would never know it had been missing.

❧ Hop on the Bus, Gus

"Mommy, where are you *going!?*" my oldest son asked me, alarmed.

The school bus was due at 8:10. I had an 8:15 appointment and had gone to start my car which was parked next to the front porch where we were waiting, so it would be ready to go as soon as the The Bigs were picked up. (My youngest went to daycare with Daddy at that time.) I had warned the office that I'd likely be a few minutes late. "As long as you're not more than ten…" the receptionist had said.

"Nowhere, honey." I called. "I'm just warming up the car."

The bus was late. I started to get annoyed, because I'd probably be pushing that ten-minute threshold. Then I thought about the bus driver. She was new. The boys told me about how they play peekaboo with her baby who goes along for the ride every day. My boys are the first on the bus so they sit up front and have ample time and opportunity to make eyes with this little girl.

I remember what it's like to get up and get going in the morning with a baby or two, and for eight crazy months before I secured a telecommuting position, three boys five and under. It's no picnic, but as the proverbial saying goes, it *does* get easier.

All their lives up until that point, I had driven the boys to daycare and/or "early start" at school first thing in the morning. Some of the time this meant I was commuting an hour plus each way up and down our local main road (our daycare is in another town, father west) before I even got to the highway. Frequently, I dialed into conference calls en route, much to the chagrin of those "Hang up and drive"-bumper-sticker people, I am sure. It was simply impossible to get my kids where they needed to be and get to the office to make a 7:30 a.m. call. And every day I had to leave work by 4:30 — thus losing valuable "face time" — in order to make the 5:30 pick up. My commute home sometimes included a late concall or at the very least, several calls to check the traffic advisory to make sure I took the route that would get me to daycare on time.

Although I work at home, my kids still go to daycare and an after school program, because I can't work around them during business hours. (And anyone who thinks differently is welcome to take them to his office for the day and see how productive he is.)

As I rejoined my children on the porch, the bus was turning down our street.

I put my arm around my oldest and pulled him close as I bent over to whisper in his ear. "I would never leave you — you know that, right?" *At least not until you're ready for me to…*I added to myself.

He blinked and gave me a small nod as I ushered him and his brother across the street and onto the bus.

❧ Remind Me Why

One Sunday, I congratulated myself because we were only six minutes late for Sunday School (which is not *really* late, since there's a singalong that precedes class). The reason we were late at all is because my middle son wanted to bring the artwork he had begun creating so he'd have something to do during the church service, but in all the pandemonium of getting out the door — which results from my kids ignoring my twenty-minute and ten-minute warnings, and then trying to cram their accessory gathering, shoes-on, tooth-brushing, hair plastering to their heads (because they refuse to maintain their buzzcuts and are now dealing with the resulting bedhead) into two minutes after I issued their final warning — he lost the pencil he was using.

I ushered my other two out to the car and prepared to deal with the maelstrom of my middle son, who had thrown himself face down on the couch, since his day was now "ruined." Another pencil would not do, it had to be *that* pencil.

I don't remember how I got him into the car, but I made sure he was in the wayback, far away from his brothers. When we arrived, I hauled him out and herded him towards the church. Lo and behold, didn't I spy *that* pencil, sticking out of his pocket. That didn't stop him from resuming his face-down position on the couch in the fellowship hall rather than partic-ipating in the singalong — he had shifted into morose mode.

My oldest is apparently too cool for singalongs now, thus he parked himself on a bench next to Grandma. My youngest charged into the unattended nursery.

I sent The Bigs to Sunday School, and then spent the time between 9:15 and 10:00 trying to convince my youngest to go to class, that the nursery is for babies. He told me he wanted to be a baby, he wanted to wear dia-pers again (not an appealing thought for me, after my near decade of diapers), and he wanted his lovey, which had been left at home when he assured me he'd just take his stuffed dog. He insisted we go back home.

"Yes, of course, honey, we'll go home after church." (I guess I'd be defer-ring that trip to the supermarket.)

During this time, The Bigs emerged from Sunday School and I sent them up to church to sit with Grandma. My youngest cried for about ten minutes, as I held him and rocked him. After I convinced him to put his thumb in his mouth, we went upstairs to the sanctuary, where I continued to rock him. My oldest had a red balloon that he was inflating and deflating repeatedly — annoying but fortunately silent. My middle son was happy to be working on his drawing again.

I can't say now what the theme of church was or what the sermon was about. I know we talked about a world mission offering and Jesus washing his disciples' feet. I remember one of the hymns. Mostly I sat there wondering why I even bother to take my kids to church.

But I know the answer. Why I bother is because it's what we do on Sundays. I can't imagine that one day when my boys are ten and up I'd start bringing them to church and expect them to sit still for an hour or two and like it, or have any clue about what's going on, or want to be there more than their Sunday morning cartoons or sports.

Why I bother is so that when they get older they will know how to take communion and why we do it (and someday they stop rolling their bread into little balls and dropping them in their little cups).

Why I bother is so they will know the songs we sing and the stories in the Bible: so they can tell their friend while playing Legos, that after we die we live forever in heaven and so they can explain to me over Sunday dinner who Shadrach, Meshach, and Abednego are.

Why I bother is so they will know there's a place they can go where people know their names, where they are loved and understood — no matter what.

Why I bother is that I promised to bring them up in the "nurture and teachings of the Lord" when they were babies, and this is a tough job to do all by myself.

That day, I left church feeling like it was worth it, even if the only reason I went to church was to have that cup of coffee and conversation with one of my loving and understanding friends who has been-there-done-that and can validate me — no matter what.

❧ Lost

Although some stores kick off the "holiday season" on or before Halloween, we waited until the day after Thanksgiving to go to a Christmas theme park.

At times during the day, I wondered why we did this. It was freezing cold; the lines were very long — to get in, to go on rides, to get food, to go to the bathroom.

My oldest wanted desperately to go on the roller coaster, having deemed the sleigh ride and the train (which we rode twice because there was no line), "boring" and "a baby ride" respectively.

We broke up the day with visits to the indoor play place and the reindeer barn, and finally, it was just time to go. But we couldn't leave without that roller coaster ride.

We had waited in line for only five minutes before my middle son started doing the "peepee dance." (He doesn't like fast rides.)

I was torn.

Could he wait until we went on the ride? (No.)

Could he go by himself — "See the restroom right up the hill over there?" (No.)

If I left the line, could my oldest manage my youngest? (No.)

So, I ran up the hill carrying my youngest, behind my middle son, leaving my oldest in line with his cell phone. I decided I might as well use the ladies' room while I was there, and I told him as I propelled him into the men's room, "Let's meet right here by this water fountain," which is a common rendezvous spot any time we split up to go potty. We do it that way everywhere from local attractions to Disneyland. So, when he wasn't there when my youngest and I emerged from the ladies' room, we just waited. And waited. And waited.

I became anxious. I saw other people coming out of the men's room. I asked one boy, who looked to be about 12, "Did you see a boy in there with a blue jacket and a red hat and gloves?"

"Nope."

My oldest called me, telling me urgently that he was almost to the head of the line. I walked *into* the men's room with my free hand over my eyes, calling for my son. He was not there. Panic set in.

I ran back down to the roller coaster ride so I could ensure that my oldest got on the ride okay.

As I rolled my eyes towards the heavens in a silent prayer, I spotted my missing son through the chain-link fence halfway up the hill I had just run down, where he had the perfect vantage point to see the roller coaster descend the first big hill.

I was so relieved, I couldn't even be mad at him.

I called and waved to him. He waved back, smiling. My youngest and I joined my oldest on the ride, and when it was over and we reunited, my middle son told me. "I was not lost, I was right there the whole time, Mama."

"Of course you were, honey." And I thanked God that our roles weren't reversed with him frantically searching for me.

❧ The Naughty and Nice List

"What if there was a 'Naughty and Nice' list, Mommy?" my oldest asked me. We were in the living room enjoying our daily holiday season viewing of *The Polar Express*.

"What do you mean, honey — not either-or, but naughty *and* nice at the same time?"

"Yeah. But that wouldn't be possible…" he said, dismissing the thought. He saw the world in black and white.

"Well, hold on just a minute — remember the coal…?" It was in a decorative dish on the side table in our dining room.

The year before I had stopped in at the oil company to see if I could have a few lumps of coal. I had been planning to tell the kids that if they didn't knock off their "Gimme-that-it's-mine-shut-up-poopy-idiot-*whack*" behavior, that's what Santa would bring them for Christmas instead of presents. I thought I might even add a few pieces to their stockings.

I'd waited for the office manager to pause in her conversation with an older gentleman. "Uhmmmmm… do you mind if I pick up a few pieces of coal from the shed?"

She laughed politely. She herself has children, so I am sure she knew what I was thinking. However, not at all amused, the man sitting with her said gravely, "Oh, no! I got coal once when I was a kid and I'm still in therapy over it!"

After hearing and pondering this, I knew it wouldn't be a good idea to attempt to control my kids' behavior with threats of coal. Besides, it would ultimately be meaningless when they received the stockings full of treats and the presents under our tree that Santa had promised them in the letters he had already sent. I wasn't going to be the one to shake their belief and trust in Santa Claus. And what did they know about coal, anyway? When we barbecue it's with a gas grill and we heat our house with oil.

Nevertheless, I did take several pieces of coal, and put them on a festive red plate in the center of our dining room table. Quite the conversation piece they were.

"What's that?"
"Where'd you get that?"
"Is that chocolate?"
"Ooo-ooo-oooh, chockit!"

"Oh, no! Don't put that in your mouth!" I snatched a hunk out of my youngest's little fist. "It's coal, boys. It's supposedly what Santa Claus brings to naughty children. Remember?" Their eyes grew wide.

But I couldn't bear to let them squirm for too long.

"Don't worry, boys. I am 100% certain that Santa is not going to — nor would he ever — bring you coal. You don't have to be perfectly good to deserve presents. We all mess up sometimes. Let's just try not to be any more naughty than we've been. Deal?"

"Deal!" They quickly agreed, obviously relieved.

"Now go and wash before we eat, please."

The next year I'd put the coal out again as a reminder that it's never too late for a "do-over."

"Yeah — I'd be on the 'Naughty *and* Nice' list," my middle son interjected. He knew I'd about reached my limit with his recent bad language and name calling. He was the child for whom, when filling out his kindergarten paperwork the year before, I'd answered "Potty Talk" in response to "other languages spoken in the home?"

I ruffled his overgrown blond buzzcut. "We all would, angel. We all would."

✣ Ringing in the New

It was New Year's Day and we were in the middle of our second snow-storm in two days. My youngest son was still napping and my older two were out for a walk with Grandma, who had come over with her dog, since the sidewalks weren't clear where she lives. I figured I'd seize the opportunity for a power nap.

I was tired from shoveling the heavy wet snow the day before, which was especially dense at the end of the driveway where the plow had deposited it.

I was worn-out from putting Christmas away (long overdue since we had begun celebrating it when we were still eating Halloween candy) in time for our New Year's Eve party.

I was drained because said party did indeed go until past midnight, even though all our friends had already left by then, because the boys *insisted* they had to see the crystal ball descend.

I was exhausted because during the first half of the New Year's Day storm, we had gone sledding over at the library playground, in between my morning and afternoon shoveling sessions.

As soon as I bade adieu to the boys and Grandma, I made a beeline for the couch and face-planted. Even though I knew I'd have 15 minutes max, those 15 minutes were mine. At last!

I closed my eyes tight and relived the holiday season and all that it entailed — incessant serial demands for special-order snacks, requests for assistance with batteries-not-included-more-than-some-assembly-required presents from Santa, and the onslaught of multiple joyful and exciting celebrations punctuated by the whining, griping, and squabbling that happens when people get over-stimulated, overwhelmed, and overtired. I was looking forward to the structure and regularity of school-and-work days.

Just as I started to drift off, a cell phone rang. Not my cell phone with its no-nonsense beep-beep-beep-beep, or Grandma's with its soothing new-agey chimes, but the kids' cell phone with its jazzy-pop ringtone, which was left on the coffee table. *Please, just let it be a text,* so I'd only hear the cadence once. But no. It went onandonandon.

Sigh. I had gone wireless years ago, and had decided to get the kids their own phone, thus empowering them to make and receive calls without using *my* cell phone, which to me is even less desirable then letting them use my laptop. The kids' phone had been mostly commandeered by my oldest. At his age, he's a relatively early adopter, but a handful of his friends do have their own phones, too, and it has been interesting to see his phone manners and messaging skills progress.

Ironically, just then my nap was thoroughly thwarted by the barrage of yet another jingle. *How clever of my son to choose a different melody for his voicemail notification*, I groused and hauled myself off the couch.

Shuffling into the kitchen to pour a cup of leftover coffee, I couldn't help but smile, though, as I recalled the text I had received from him just that morning: "Iloveyou" plus an animated GIF emoticon with hearts popping out of its eyes. The message would remain locked not only on my phone, but also in my heart.

❧ "Rich" is a Relative Term

"Mommommom! Pick a color!" My middle son thrust a cootie-catcher at me. I was folding laundry on the dining room table.

"Orange."

He studied the word momentarily and then spelled out, "O-R-A-N-G-E." as he worked his fingers back and forth, opening the cootie catcher first one way and then the other, six times to correspond with the letters in the word "orange."

"Pick a number." He showed me the number choices inside the cootie catcher.

"Two."

"One-two." He moved the cootie catcher back and forth again.

"Okay, pick another number. This is your *final* number…" he said gravely, to underscore that I should choose wisely.

"Five."

He lifted the flap where the number five was written so he could tell me my fortune. "You are rich," he announced with a big smile.

"Ummmm…well…" and my mind wandered to my post-Christmas credit card bills and to the camp brochures that had arrived the previous week necessitating that I begin planning how to finance my summer childcare plans. And then to the oil delivery that was certainly imminent because it had been so cold that winter, save for that one week where we had a couple of 50-degree days. I lamented that my grocery budget seemed out of control and that every morning I counted out small coins (doing my best to limit the number of pennies because my oldest had informed me that nobody at school has time to count pennies) for milk money.

"…do you think we're rich, honey?"

"Of course, Mom. You have alotta money!"

I smiled back at him and reflected with much gratitude that my boys don't know what it's like not to get relief from their hunger or cold, and that they weren't yet too cool to shun hand-me-downs. And that we had made it through the year that I coughed up one-third of my income for childcare — and all that entailed. That year there were times that I wondered why I bothered working at all, and cursed the powers-that-be that I could only claim $5K of that money as tax exempt — don't "they" know that if I didn't have childcare, I wouldn't be able to contribute to the economy at all?

"Hmmmm. 'Alotta' isn't exactly a number, but it's enough to get most of what we need and some of what we want…" I contemplated how one year rebuilding the front porch trumped our vacation plans, but the next year the trip to Disney and some white duct tape kept our bathroom on the deferred maintenance program.

The boys and I frequently talk about needs vs. wants. I remind them of one of my favorite sayings, "Happiness is not having everything you want, but wanting everything you have."

"…so, if you think we're rich, we are," I confirmed.

People often say to me, "God bless you," when they find out I have three sons. This usually occurs when they witness me herding them through the supermarket, church, or the airport when I flew them across the country to visit Grandma and back. I tell them, "He already has." Richly.

❧ I'll Take a Rain Check

The dreaded phone call came at five-something a.m. *Please, please, please let it just be a delay.* But no. School was *closed*. I snapped my phone shut, cutting off the cheerful recorded message. *Hmmmmph!* Tossing the covers back, I bolted out of bed and peeked through the drapes.

It was only raining but Main Street was a mess. *Okay, I see the logic,* but that didn't change the fact that I had five conference calls and two offsite meetings scheduled that day, plus numerous bordering-on-late action items that I knew would have to wait until my third shift.

Grandma had been pressed into service each of the two nights previously, to spare me from dragging my trio to back-to-back den meetings. With a tinge of guilt, I asked her again to come over.

"That's what Grandmas are for," she said. "What time to you need me?"

I went out to shovel the slush to prepare for her arrival and my departure. *Boy, this has been a tough season,* I lamented as I sloshed through my driveway. *I hate winter!* Water had started leaking through my boots. "Q@#%* rain!" I cursed aloud, as I realized my jacket wasn't completely waterproof, either.

Fortunately there were no little ears nearby as my kids have been known to repeat select phrases far out of context. They were snug and cozy in the house, having been up (ironically) since the crack of dawn — gleefully watching cartoons in their jammies, ensconced on the couch with pillows, blankies, and the muffins I'd made the night before.

"Because, boys, Mommy has *work* to do!" was my reply when they asked me, as they did every single time we had a "weather day," why I don't like school closings. I could not remember when we last had a full week of school. Oh, maybe it was back in October sometime when my kids were serially sick, necessitating that at least one of them was home with me for the majority of the week.

The banging on the window interrupted my reverie. I looked up to see my oldest pantomiming with his empty cup that he needed refill.

"Get it yourself or wait!" I sang forcefully, a smile frozen over my clenched teeth.

I turned my attention back to the job at hand. I needed to find the silver lining. *Thank God I didn't have to do this yesterday!* I'd had an 8:30 a.m. meeting in the city. *At least I won't need to worry about childcare during the now-nonexistent week between school and camp.* I pulled my phone out of my pocket and amiably rescheduled my midday meeting. *And who would blame me for skipping that 5 p.m. call since most normal people are preparing to conclude business at that time?*

With both my attitude and schedule lightened and with Grandma's help, I made it through my work day, only occasionally counting the hours until bedtime.

Finally, 8:00 and my turn to be gleeful. "Time for bed, boys — Mommy's tired!"

Soon I was parked on the couch with my laptop, answering email, juggling my calendar, re-checking weather.com, and…dozing off. Since my work would be there the next day but the weather wouldn't, I took a rain check.

❧ When the Rubber Hits the Road

One time we were headed to the early start program at the elementary school cafeteria. The shortest route to the entrance of the café is to go around the building to the right, which is the way I always went, usually without incident. On that day, however, a woman coming out as I was going in was gesticulating angrily at me. I cringed, because technically she's right. There's a big "Do Not Enter" sign on that particular path.

I used to obey that sign and drive all the way around to the left, between the middle school and elementary school, past the playground, then along the track — basically 270 degrees around a circle.

But I'm all for simple when it comes to morning routines, and since I soon realized that lots of people disregard that sign, it wasn't long before I justified ignoring it too.

Though, it did nag at my conscience a bit. It especially hit home when one of The Bigs pointed out, "Mommy, doesn't that sign say 'Do Not Enter'?"

"Why, yes it does. Good reading!"

Silence. *What was he thinking?* I could only imagine how his brain processed this tidbit of data.

This is the same rules-based, literal-minded son with whom I debated as we were leaving the library playground one day.

"Mommy, what does 'No Thru Traffic' mean?"

"Well, honey, in this case, it means you can't cut through here from abc street to Main."

"Well, Mah-ahm! Then why are we going this way?"

"Well, honey-ee. We're not "cutting through." We came from there, stopped here, now we have to go to the post office. So we're going up to Main Street. You don't really think I should go back that way, then all the way around to xyz street, since the abc hill is one way and then hummina-hummina-hummina" at this point was surely all he heard of my excuse.

He answered, "Yes. It says 'No Thru Traffic' so don't go through."

But I did anyway.

It was when I became a parent that things like wearing a seatbelt and crossing in the cross walk; actually sitting at the dinner table and using the manners my own parents drilled into me; and going to church on Sundays became more than just theoretical, nice, and in some cases, law-abiding, things to do.

Had I let him down? This thought haunted me until the morning not long after, we followed one of the school administrators going "the wrong way" into the cafeteria parking lot.

"Oh, look, boys, isn't that Ms. So-and-so?"

Glancing away from his Game Boy briefly, my middle son answered "Uhm…yeah…"

"Hmmm. Well…if *Ms. So-and-so* can go this way, it *must* be okay — right?" I rationalized.

"I guess," he replied, without taking his eyes off Yoshi's Island.

I have to ask myself, though, when the rubber hits the road, am I setting the right example for my kids? Just because everyone else does it, does that make it right? If all my friends jumped off a bridge…

❧ Scratch That

Our pastor and I were talking about my middle son making the bread for communion during our Holy Thursday service. A nearby grandma said, "Oh, what a wonderful thing to do — I used to make knot rolls and braided baguettes with my kids!"

I looked at her blankly before I realized she was talking about making bread from scratch — mixing, kneading, punching, squeezing, forming, and baking. I am not unfamiliar with the concept — I have, in fact, done it that way as a child, with my own mom.

Sure, and my mom used to sew a lot of our clothes, too. I don't even like to sew on buttons. One year, I felt particularly triumphant when I paid the dry cleaner to sew the patches on my son's Tiger Cub uniform, until someone clued me in to Badge Magic™, the revolutionary new way to attach badges to Scout uniforms without sewing — it's peel-and-stick badge adhesive.

I had to fess up that I intended to use our newly acquired bread machine to make the communion bread, and that once I put the ingredients in, I wasn't planning to open up the machine (and I admonish the kids about this very fact) until they turn into bread.

My middle son is a selective eater, and when he had devoured the bread at one of my friends' Sunday dinners, I was so excited about the fact that he tried something new, and liked it, that I made my request on our freecycle list — and got the bread machine the very same week. An additional bonus is that now he and I have a special activity to share.

On the morning of Holy Thursday I supervised while my son measured the ingredients and poured them all into the bread machine. It took all of about ten minutes, including our discussion about The Last Supper, and then he was off while the bread machine did its thing.

In comparison, the scratch method would have taken hours. Sure, we'd get breaks when the dough rose, but by then my son would already be in school and I'd be an hour into my work day.

Our busy schedules and the ease of automation and/or pre-packaged baking mixes are all I need to justify not baking from scratch. Muffins?

Empty mix into bowl and add water. Cookies? Tear apart the little refrigerated dough squares. And everyone has always loved my cake and brownies — thank you very much Betty and Duncan. As one of my colleagues confirmed, "If it comes out of your oven, it's homemade."

My mom has pointed out that boxed mixes really only save you a few steps — since the ingredients are in my cabinets anyway...

"Time is money, Mother." I interrupted.

..."While more than doubling the cost," she replies.

Hmmmph!

At church one time, my youngest was eating a sliver of chocolate bundt cake with white confectioner's glaze. He delivered the following news with a smile and a song: "Dishes beddadin yo-was."

I gasped. *Better than mine?* "Can I get you a napkin, honey?" I marched over to the kitchen window in the fellowship hall. "Okay, who made this delicious cake?" I asked the ladies serving refreshments. "I simply *must* have the recipe."

That was years ago, though, and I never did get around to trying the recipe.

❧ Life is a Highway

"Are we on the high road?" my almost-three-year old asked me.

"What's that, honey?" I glanced up at the rear view mirror. We were on a numbered route, but it was still a two-lane road.

"The high road. Are we on the high road, Mom?"

"Oh! You mean the highWAY!" I chuckled, emphasizing the second syllable of the word.

My mind wandered back to "the high road," though. I told the kids all the time — not in so many words — to take the high road.

"It doesn't matter who started it, don't hit your brother. Walk away, walk away — just walk away!"

"Boys, I don't care who made that mess — it needs be cleaned up before you can watch TV. All of you. Teamwork."

"Okay, if you can't share that toy, I'll have a turn with it," which means it goes into toy abeyance, possibly forever in the case of certain weapons or party-favor-bag tchotchkes.

Frequently I am at a crossroads with my children.

"Why don't *you* just walk away?"
I am, see me going?

"How come you're not helping? You never do anything around here!"
God help me, and my eyes roll towards the heavens.

"You're the meanest mom in the whole world! I hate you."
I can't say that I have *never* taken the low road and suggested that they go find a nicer mom to live with, but more often than not, the offender is required to take a break in his room. "Honey, you can feel however you want. But you may not speak to me that way."

The time out is just as important for me as my child: similar to a road trip, sometimes you've got to pull into a rest stop and consult the map, or you might end up on an unexpected and unwelcome detour.

This same plan serves me well when dealing with the business associate who may have inadvertently (or not) made my job more difficult; the friend I've caught in a social lie; that guy suddenly in line in front of us at the baseball game; the driver who can't use a turn signal because her hand is busy holding her phone up to her ear; or any tactlessly honest people who feel compelled to bless me with their opinions ("Mom, you're like, *so old!*"). Smile and walk away, walk away — just walk away.

One day I almost missed the exit for the high road when, even after a time out, I was still fuming about the hole in the wall at the bottom of the stair-well: the hole that got there when someone rolled a 10-pound dumbbell down the stairs, even after someone had been told that we don't push toys, suitcases, or *anything* down the stairs. Ever.

My eyeballs may as well have been popping out and my ears blasting steam I was so close to boiling over. But, I shelved my own feelings, because they weren't as important as my almost-three-year old with the tearfully imploring eyes and the trembling frown learning that "Mommy still loves me even when she's mad and she will forgive me when I say I am sorry."

"Yeah, the highway. Are we?" he pressed.

"Well, not really…"

"Then why are we going so fast?"

I promptly removed my foot from the accelerator, grateful that the guy I was tailgating apparently *was* on the high road.

✒ Summertime, and the Living Is Easy

"Get away, Mom!" My middle son snarled and shrugged away from my embrace, as though he were disgusted. I had just hugged and kissed his older brother goodbye and now I was bidding him farewell as I dropped them off at summer camp.

I tried not to take it personally, but still my heart skipped a beat.

I put my hand on his shoulder and said, "See you this afternoon," and turned around and walked out the recreation center door, heading back down the hill to my car.

I know that our primary goal as parents is to prepare our children to grow up and become independent, while evolving into educated, civilized, and productive members of society. The latter part of that statement is something of which I remind them frequently when they gripe loudly about school or chores, the former I let slide. They still think they are going to live with me forever. My oldest has asked me what is the closest college to our house; my youngest thinks that when he rescues his girlfriend from the castle, "she's gonna live with us at our house, Mom!"

My middle son's outburst of autonomy took me by surprise. I remember not long ago when I had one or both of my older boys clinging to my legs at daycare, insisting "I don WAN go!" Or my oldest telling me he needed the thermometer (in order to convince me he was sick.)

I would peel them off and hand them over to a teacher, who would coax them to say goodbye and blow kisses to me out the window. One would be sobbing and would refuse to look at me. The other would try to comply, but he just looked weary.

"I love you both," I said, pressing my nose against the window screen. And with false bravado: "I'll see you at 6:00 — have a great day!" I didn't want them to see me cry.

But I did, for most of the 30-plus miles I drove to work. Twenty minutes or so into the ride I'd pull myself together to call daycare to make sure my boys were alright (they always were); then sniff and sob intermittently *because* they were, and I was the one with the emotional hangover. And at the end of the workday, I'd be praying I'd get to daycare in time that my kids wouldn't be the last ones there, or even worse that I'd be paying the dollar-a-minute late fee times two.

"Mommommom," I heard my middle son calling out the sliding screen door of the camp recreation center.

I looked up the hill.

"Bye, Mom!"

I smiled and blew him two kisses and gave him a thumbs up.

He tapped his chest and then gave me back a peace sign, a thumbs up, and then an "I love you," sign, which is basically a thumbs up and "Rock on!" combined, the same hand signs we shared during the school year after he'd boarded the bus on a good day. (If it was the worst day of his life, I'd just get a thumbs-down.).

And rock on I did, smiling at my son as I returned the signs. After all, it was summer time and we had survived the final two weeks of school during which we had been inundated not only with rain, resulting in a couple of baseball playoff game reschedules, but also with special requests from the room parents, teachers, and school for summer-birthday-celebration pizza parties; lost library book fees; class play rehearsals before and after school; payment for the 2nd set of class pictures (which I had to buy because I needed pictures for the scrap book pages that the room parents were making for the teachers); teacher gift contributions; food donations for the class parties; a used book for the book buddy book swap; and signed permission slips to allow continued pen pal communications over the summer (not likely to happen since it's hard enough to get anyone to write thank-you notes).

There were no more sports practices, scout meetings, or homework. No more making lunches every morning (except for my youngest whose preschool routine remained unchanged since he was still too young for camp at that time); the camp provides lunch. All the kids had to remember was a bathing suit and towel. All I had to remember was sunscream. My commute was simply back to my home office, since I'd held a telecommuting position for the past three years.

Yes, it's summertime, and the living is easy…

❧ Human Doing

"Don't make me stop this car…" I said with a stern look in the rearview mirror.

"Snicker, snicker, snort…" was the reply I got.

"I'm not kidding boys — there are a lot of things I'd rather be doing right now…"

We were on our way to pick up my youngest at daycare, two towns to the west, after having been at a dual doctor visit, in another town to the north, racing against the clock so I could get the kids home, fed, and started on their homework before Grandma came over so I could go to curriculum night. Their pent-up energy (from practicing their doctor's office manners for far too long) was escaping.

Or maybe it was the time that my oldest was kicking my seat and whacking his brother because he didn't like my explanation of why at ages eight and seven, they can't stay alone in the house while I pick their brother up from daycare early, so we can make our two 5:00 soccer practices — that happen to be miles apart in two different towns (neither of which are anywhere near daycare).

Oh, wait, maybe we were on our way from daycare to McDonald's, after I dragged my older two out of Extended Day early — "Awwww mom, I'm not done with my turn on the computer" — where soon I'd be admonishing my middle son to stop poking his brother with his Happy Meal toy and stay focused on eating so he'd have time to change into his Cub Scout uniform, en route to his den meeting.

I guess I'm not sure when it was exactly that this conversation occurred, it could have been any time my kids were in the back seat of my car. But what I haven't forgotten is what my oldest asked me and the fact that I was stumped.

"What *would* you rather be doing, Mom?"

I had become so enmeshed in the back-to-school-sports-scouts-activity-homework hubbub that *I didn't have a clue!*

⚓ Shirts and Skins

"I wan a diff'rent shirt," my youngest sobbed. He had torn off his new Superman pajama shirt and cape with the flashing emblem — that he had insisted on wearing — in a fit of pique because I made him get out of the car. My hauling him like a screaming octopus onto the soccer field — just barely in time for the game — made for a grand entrance.

"I hear you, honey. You want a different shirt."

"I juss wah ah ahnt a diff rent shir irh irht."

"After the game you can have a different shirt."

"I want it NOW!"

"We're at soccer now."

"No! I WANT IT NOW!" he screamed and flailed and arched his back.

I could feel people all around us staring. He was shouting louder than any of them were cheering. *Why was I even trying to reason with an agitated three-year-old?*

Ironically, just the day before I had suggested to a colleague, whose daughter refuses to wear a coat, "Just let her wear whatever she wants. She'll realize soon enough that she's cold." My colleague was concerned with what other parents might think. "They'll understand when you flash the coat at them."

Another soccer mom tried to jolly my son up. When he refused her offer of the blanky she was sitting on, she inviting him to play soccer with her four year old. "C'mon, we'll be shirts — you be skins."

It felt good to laugh: it had become a challenge to remember the advice I had given my colleague.

After the game, I took a deep breath and plastered a smile on my face before returning the jacket that my son had reluctantly accepted from his four-year-old buddy. The dad reassured me, "We all knew what was going on."

✑ NapQuest

"What in the world was that buzzing noise?"

I opened one eye and it took a moment or two to realize where I was, when it was, and what I was doing: trying to take a nap on the couch one afternoon. My older two were with their dad and my youngest was having a much-needed siesta on the adjacent couch. My phone shimmied across the coffee table as it continued to vibrate. I snatched it up, looked at it and tossed it back on the table disgustedly, as I didn't recognize the number. I figured whoever it was would leave a voicemail.

I squeezed my eyes shut again to block out the sunny day it had become after the overcast morning that we had all spent at one of the baseball diamonds at the town field. I had alternated as pitcher, catcher, umpire, and arbitrator during our family baseball game. My younger two, who had got up far too early (in my opinion), had short fuses and I realized we better head home since we'd need the last of their energy reserves to make it back home on the rail trail. The boys had all ridden their bicycles, and it was my youngest's debut on his new-to-him two wheeler with training wheels.

I couldn't drift off again, though.

As it had turned out, my youngest couldn't complete the ride — he was even slower than the notoriously pokey dog, who sniffed just about everything coming and going. I'd alternately urged my son along and towed him by the front handlebars with my left hand, but he was becoming a puddle. I told The Bigs to go ahead, and we abandoned his little bicycle on the side of the trail about a half mile from our house. And even though I had the bat bag containing all four of our baseball gloves, seven balls, as well as the bat slung over my right shoulder and our softsided lunch cooler and the dog's leash in my right hand, I scooped up my son with my left arm and hoisted him over my hip. We trudged along and when we got to the off ramp, where we'd go up the hill to our street, I set him down.

"Can you walk now, honey?"

"No, Mommy," he'd answered in a small voice.

"Okay," I'd sighed, and groaned inwardly, "just give me a minute."

Annoyed, I realized with the absence of buzzing, that whoever it was didn't even leave a voicemail: my nap was wrecked for nothing. I snatched my silent phone back up and looked at the time. I had only been asleep for 15 minutes.

Nevertheless, I lay on the couch with my arm draped over my eyes and thought about things. I thought about the spreadsheet I had planned to finish the day before; the dishes in sink and the laundry on dining room table; the two birthday parties I needed to plan; my 2nd grader's weekend homework; the various piles of papers that needed attending to, most urgently were all the forms that had come from the camp that the boys would be attending; the fact that I had to talk in church the next day (*about what,* I wondered); and lastly, I lamented the column I didn't write the week before, though I did turn out two masterfully written presentations for work and a press release for my friend's band.

I realized this could have been any typical Saturday. And indeed, hadn't it been months before when I actually started this very story, except the event preceding my napquest was my oldest's basketball evaluations during which I had held my restless youngest son in my lap on the crowded bleachers (when I wasn't taking him to the potty or to get a drink) trying to keep him amused with the contents of the purse and the jewelry I was wearing, while my middle roamed the halls of the school doing God-only-knows-what?

I had so much to do, yet I remained on the couch.

With my eyes defying daylight, my other senses were amplified. I could hear the traffic on the street and a dog barking (and was glad it was not mine: he was asleep on the other end of the small couch with my son) through the open living room windows. I shivered as the breeze wafted through the curtains and I could smell someone's freshly cut grass. And oh, I guess the mourning doves were back after all.

"Sleep when the baby sleeps." I'd heard the saying years prior when my oldest was the baby. And finally — with my third son who was going on four at the time and would insist, "Don't call me 'Baby' anymore, Mom!" — I had begun taking the advice to heart. The only challenge was that with three kids, opportunities for naps were few and far between.

As my understanding editor had said the day before, "No problem. It's good to give the brain a rest every now and then. Maybe next time."

But still I'd panicked. *What if I have writer's block? What if there was no next time? Well, what if? What if I just took a break from writing?*

But he was right. I did need a rest. I had been running on empty for far too long. Everything else could wait. It would have to.

I lingered where I was, thinking and putting things in perspective. When my son began to stir, I reached over and held his hand at the right angle where the matching couches met. We lay in companionable silence for a good while.

Then, "Are you ready to go get your bike?"

"Okay, Mommy."

Refreshed, we started over. What might have seemed like a waste, was actually a good investment of time.

❧ Doing God's Work

I was catching up with a friend on the phone. I'd been really busy with additional responsibilities at work, and thus did not have the luxury to monotask, so I figured I'd return the call while I was walking the dog. My friend was telling me about the Wall Street guy and his Ponzi scheme.

"Wait. What?…" I interrupted. "Did you say millions or billions?" I had been preoccupied, wondering when the dog was going to poop.

"Billions," he replied, and proceeded to explain this guy's role in the fall of our national economy.

"But the economy will right itself," I told him. "Surely you've heard about the economic theory of equilibrium?" *Gosh, I hope the dog poops soon, because I have a conference call in 25 minutes.*

Next he began a diatribe about people who had lost their life savings.

"Uhmmm, isn't there some sort of investment protection insurance? I'm sure those people are gonna get their money back…" *Hmmm…do I actually have two conference calls back to back? With all these calls, how am I ever going to get any work done? I have a project overdue and I need to help the kids with their homework tonight. If the dog doesn't poop now, I am not going to have time to walk him again before I have to go get the kids. I can't be late for the kids. And when am I going to finish that project. God, help me. I think we'll be having "Breakfast Night" for dinner again tonight…geez, I still have to figure out what I am going to talk about on Sunday for the invocation…maybe "worrying" would be a good topic.*

So that's what I talked about. We all worry. If we are not worrying about our physiological needs (food, water, shelter, safety), we are worried about our psychological needs (friendship, achievement, self-actualization). Or we might worry about much broader issues like social change, the economy, Mr. Ponzi, and other things going on in the world.

I decided to survey my kids. "Boys, what do you worry about?"

My oldest answered, "Nothing. I don't want to say it. Okay, tests in school and that I'm gonna get a bad grade. Oh, yeah, and I'm worried about the Pinewood Derby." He had just returned from the weigh in.

My middle son asked, "What do you mean? Why — are you gonna put that in the newspaper? It's private. I worry about stuff. Okay?" (I know what he's worried about, and like he said, it's private.)

My youngest, answered, "My brothers. When they sass me."

"Is anyone worried about the economy?" I asked.
"What's the economy?"

"Well, how about this — do you obsess about anything?"
My middle son quipped, "The Pinewood Derby, the Pinewood Derby, the Pinewood Derby."

"Yes, that would be obsessing. Okay, let's see. Does anything keep you up at night?"
"My brother snoring!" was one son's reply. His two brothers said in unison, "I don't snore!"

We all laughed.

Sometimes worry has positive effects, if it prompts us to take precautions, like wearing seatbelts or studying for tests and to avoid risky behaviors, like skydiving or pulling the dog's tail. However, worrying too much — especially over things that we can't control — can cause high blood pressure, ulcers, and all manner of health problems.

Personally, I don't spend a lot of time thinking about those broader issues — the types of things one might hear on the news, because I don't watch the news. I can't afford to add tragedy, scandal, and gossip to everything else that concerns me right under my own roof, like grocery shopping, homework, laundry, sports, scouts, playdates, and so on. If something important is going on in the world, I know I will hear about it through friends, as I did Mr. Ponzi.

There was one day not long ago that I had such a hard time with work that my stomach was in knots, I was chewing my cuticles, and I wasn't breathing deeply enough. I had to get up a few times and walk away from my computer and pray — out loud — to take myself out of panic mode, remembering an email blessing I'd received from a friend, "The will of God will never take you where the Grace of God will not protect you."

Then I called to mind other good advice. "Don't sweat the small stuff." According to my mom, "It's all small stuff."

"At least you have a job," pointed out a job-hunting friend. "Right," I agreed and reminded myself that since worrying is God's work, I really need to stop doing His job in addition to my own newly expanded-because-of-layoffs job. *I'm grateful for a lot of things, especially my job — that's how I afford the roof in the first place.*

🐍 Homework, Homework — Gimme a Break!

"What's up, Carlie?" my friend asked one Saturday.

"Oh, not much, really," I said, trying to manage the phone and wield my glue stick simultaneously. "I'm just doing my son's homework."

"What? You sound muffled." This is always the case when I shoulder the phone. "It sounded like you said you were *doing* his homework."

"Well, I am," I said, capping the glue stick, sitting up straight and pushing my chair back from the table. "Kind of…"

"You're doing it? Or you're helping him do it?"

I got up and started pacing, which I often do when I'm on the phone. "Well, he already did the work part. I'm just gluing it all to the poster-board. When he started weeping and wailing and gnashing his teeth, I sent him outside."

I peeked out the window at my son, who was making snow angels in the back yard.

"Hmmmph. I don't know…" my friend said skeptically.

"I do. He did the research and writing. I don't think he's gonna get graded on cutting and pasting, and he just couldn't deal anymore."

Neither could I, practically. I had ignored this project over Thanksgiving break, Christmas break and every weekend in between, since I simply didn't want our family time consumed with my 2nd grader's homework. *He* didn't want his family time consumed by his homework. He has far more homework than his third-grade brother (who rubs it in any chance he can get). But still, I wondered, *Was I helping too much?*

The next day another friend called me, "Hi Carlie, what are you doing?"

"Oh, my son's homework…well, I'm just putting together the presentation really…" I started to explain.

She interrupted me. "Yeah, I know how it is. I think the teacher expects the parents to do some of it, at least until the kids are more independent."

I felt better to hear her say that and so hoped it was true. Not only did I not want to be a stage mother to my son's schoolwork but also, I couldn't envision another 10 years of enduring homework meltdowns, "working dinners," or finishing homework while waiting for the school bus.

Though, I sometimes wonder if I will ever have the opportunity to use those two years of calculus I was forced to take in high school.

❧ Silent Night

I actually like Christmas Eve better than Christmas. For one thing, my three sons are usually compliant about going to bed because they want to make it as easy as possible for Santa. They know he won't come if they're awake.

What seals the deal for us is the "Reindeer Food" we get every year from a friend at church.

I read the "directions for use" out loud to my boys. "Prior to going to bed, sprinkle the reindeer food on the ground. Run back into the house, brush your teeth, say your prayers and jump into bed. Go right to sleep."

It's the one night a year I don't have to argue with them about 8:00 bedtime. *Grown up time, at last!*

All is calm.

Another thing is, there's a certain feeling of contentment in knowing that I have done all there is to do — or at least all that can be done. The presents are wrapped and under the tree. The gifts and cards are sent out, and the ones that aren't will become New Year's greetings. The frenzy of the previous weeks — list making, purchasing, organizing, hiding, baking, planning, executing…everything — is done, whether it's done as planned or not. The clock has run down.

All is bright.

To me, Christmas Eve is the high point prior to the denouement that the actual holiday is. I try not to think about the fact that the gift opening lasts merely minutes followed closely by the burrowing through wrapping paper, hunting hopefully for something that just might have been overlooked. Then comes the bouncing off the walls, arguing, grabbing, and demanding to know when our extended family is coming over with more presents.

Sleep in heavenly peace.

The house is clean and quiet. Church was attended. The cookies and note for Santa are left on the table. I take a picture of the tree with the gifts under it, decorated on the top half only by this time, as is the tree in any household with young children who like to pull off anything within reach, sometimes leaving dirty socks or empty juice boxes instead.

I know that my admonition to wait until it's light out before we get up fell on deaf ears, so I can't stay up too late. If the clock on the wall next to the tree (which is always included in my picture) reads 10:30, I'm doing alright.

I bask in the tranquil moments as I share some of Santa's cookies, and survey the slim tree snug in the corner of our smallish dining room. At last, all is well.

Sleep in heavenly peace.

❧ One Day They'll Thank Me

"You didn't go to the store yet? We're almost out of milk!"
"I had a busy day, boys. We can go on the way back from the den meeting." (I was lucky to get the laundry done, changing it between machines during breaks in my workday, and folding it during a conference call.)

"Chicken and smiley fries again?"
"Yes, isn't that great? It's something you all like!" (I can't be a short order cook every night.)

"What are these piles of clothes all over my bed?"
"Clean laundry. Put it away — in your drawers — please." (Yes, I need to specify where, since sometimes the definition of "away" is anywhere but the bed.)

I don't know what my kids think I do all day. One day when we were waiting for the bus, they announced that they hadn't had time to brush their teeth. I was astounded. As I reflected on the hubbub that morning — my middle son doing his homework while eating his breakfast, my oldest doing anything he could to distract him (which was something akin to yodeling after I insisted he keep his hands to himself), and my youngest telling me he needed help with his shirt (which he did not — he needed attention), the dog and cat orbiting me, while I was trying to make the lunches and ensure everything everyone needed was laid out next to their backpacks (recorder for oldest, library books for middle, snow suit and boots for youngest), and consume enough coffee to continue functioning against the backdrop of an early morning conference call on speakerphone, I could barely wait for the bus to come. Despite how busy I might be, I still make time to brush. "But you get to stay home all day, Mommy!" my son said. He must assume I am sitting at home in my pajamas watching Nickelodeon and eating toaster pastries (which is what he would be doing if I hadn't reoriented him this morning).

"Where's my homework?"
"Did you put it in your homework drawer or is it still in your backpack?"
"I don't know. Can you get it?"
"Not right now, honey, I'm doing the dishes."
"I'm not doing it then!"
"Well, think again, 'cause I'm sure not gonna do it!"
"You never do *anything* for us!"

What is so absurd about that comment is that everything I do is for them (though I try not to do too much of their homework) or because of them. As I have stated previously, they are my "why."

"All my friends have Wii. We're like the only kids that don't have a Wii!" "You have Xbox® set up in your den in the basement! When I was a kid…" (…but I stopped myself. Anything I said would be as meaningless as my own mom's stories about how far she walked to school when she was in kindergarten were to me as a child, though they do mean something to me now.)

When I was a kid, we didn't have video games or even a color T.V. until I was a senior in high school (even though they were already invented). I had to eat whole wheat bread and yogurt and tofu before it was cool (I have not yet insulted my children with tofu, but the other items are standard fare). I wore yard sale and thrift shop clothes and we heated bricks on the woodstove that would later be wrapped in towels and slipped between our bedsheets since we turned our thermostat down to just-above-pipes-freezing every night (I still love a good bargain but the bricks are a thing of the past and likely would be even if we had a woodstove).

Are my kids ever going to appreciate how good they have it? I think it's possible when I hear a dinner prayer like the following:

"Heavenly Father, thank you for this day and our food and we went to the playground and I fell down and hurt my knee. I was the line leader in school today, and then it was library day. I got a book about SuperFly Guy. I don't really like apple but mom makes me eat it before I can have treat. Oh, yeah, and thank you that we got to go to Disney World. In Jesus Christ, Amen and a-women."

Not long after my mother passed away, I came across a thank-you card amongst her keepsakes. I had written it to her on Mother's Day the year I graduated from college. "You have given up so much and made so many sacrifices for us. I guess I've just started realizing this and I'm very grateful. And also proud. You set an example for us… Thank you for all your love and support, and sanctioning, advising, encouraging, cooking, and everything else…"

Gratitude increases as awareness grows. Maybe it will be that first time my sons do their own laundry, plan and execute a family meal, or insist that everyone stop shouting and kicking in the back of the car — it might take time, but I am sure that one day they'll thank me. I am eternally grateful to my own late mother, as the magnitude of all she has done for me continues to unfold.

❦ How I Spent My Summer Vacation

For me, there was no question about how I spent my summer vacation, it was clear each week when I wrote the checks to camp and daycare. However, if my elementary-school-aged sons were asked to write this traditional back-to-school essay, what would they say, I wondered.

We didn't have a real vacation this summer, meaning the kind where you pack things and leave your home for an extended period of time. Though I'd taken one week straight off from work and had grandiose plans for a road trip to Niagara Falls with a friend and her kids, those dwindled to going to Maine for part of the week, to simply taking day trips.

We called this our "Daycation."

One of our day trips was going to be to a large amusement park in another part of the state. We had set aside either of two days for this. Though, as the days drew near, the weather forecast was like a cold black cloud coming down. Additionally, given that it was a two hour drive (the drive time being what caused the reduction in road trip length initially: spending time in a car with three boys thrashing, poking, jockeying for position, and asking me what time is it, when are we gonna get there, how many more minutes, what does the GPS say, is highly undesirable), we chose to go to a more local amusement park on a different day altogether.

Unfortunately, it seemed that everyone else had the same plan. We had to park at a remote lot and be shuttled to the park, which meant my strategy for taking a break midday and eating the carefully prepared food I had packed went out the window. I wound up buying fried food, soda, cotton candy, ice cream and all manner of naughty and costly things.

My kids were hot and grumpy and this was one of the occasions during the week when I said out loud, "Maybe we all would've enjoyed our week more if you stayed in camp and daycare and I took a week off by myself," though I had surely thought it numerous times.

As the day wore on, the crowds thinned. My youngest and I were sitting on the Sky Ride, which is a gondola-type ride that travels high above the length of the park. I pointed out that it was a good thing we hadn't come any earlier (as the kids had lamented) or we wouldn't have been able to last all day to see the magic show and the fireworks.

"Mom, what's gravity?" he asked, ignoring my insight.

As much as I would have liked to engage in a grave discussion of amusement park physics, I told him, "Uhmmm. That's a good question for your dad, honey. He's a physicist."

We sat in comfortable silence, and I reflected on some of the life lessons that were illustrated that day. Aside from physics, and practicing patience by waiting in long lines, "black diamond" attractions at amusement parks such as roller coasters show us that life includes ups and downs, twists and turns, and sometimes an upside down part. The water park reminded us that occasionally things get dumped on you unexpectedly. Riding the Ferris Wheel was a good example of how when you're on top of the world, you can see the big picture, but when you're down in the weeds, you can only see what's in front of you. My youngest's inaugural experience on the bumper cars taught him that when you hold on too tight and try to steer things your way, you end up spinning in circles, but when you let go, you move forward with ease.

Technically, the fact that summer was a break in the usual routine — and as Dictionary.net defines a vacation: "being free from a duty or service — we had been on vacation for the whole eight weeks. (At least the kids were, as they were free from the duties of school and scouts, but my duty and service simply shifted from helping them with merit badges and homework to shuttling them to camp and summer sports. Maybe next year I will take that solo week off.)

As the season of summer wound down, we had a few more days off before the start of school. We spent these last days in a frenzy of activity — mostly baseball related, with a mix of laser tag and backyard fun with friends thrown in — before we had to settle back into our school-year routine. The kids' teachers' letters had already arrived in the mail with the foreshadowing, "I'm looking forward to hearing about your summer adventures."

❧ I Hate You! Wanna Play DS Download?

"I'm *never* gonna let go of you no matter what!" my middle son avowed to his younger brother. We were packed into our car with some friends on the way back from a three-story indoor playground, which oh-by-the-way also has video games, bowling, and amusement rides where we had spent the better part of a rainy afternoon. The visit had brought out the best and worst in the kids, and by the time I insisted we had to leave *now,* two thirds of my offspring had told me (one more than once), "I hate you, Mommy!"

There was considerable ado about the seating arrangements. Our sporty station wagon can seat seven passengers, but not as comfortably as a mini van. I had to configure and reconfigure, in order to accommodate my youngest who had collapsed on the wet ground in the parking lot when I insisted he walk the rest of the way to the car after having hauled him away — writhing like a sack of octopi — from all the riveting fun.

When he refused to buckle his seat belt in the car, or keep it buckled when I strapped him in, I asked the kids to rearrange themselves once again. "I need you," I said to my middle son. Our eyes met and he sighed and groaned as he swapped seats with one of our guests, because he understood my innuendo. I was requesting that he sit next to his brother and hold the seat belt to prevent it from being unbuckled.

My youngest wept and wailed and gnashed his teeth and tried to convince us all that his brother was hurting him; that he couldn't breathe. He howled, he moaned (thus I was sure he could, indeed, breathe). "Click it or ticket," my middle son maintained. The tension in the car was thick; our communal anxiety was high. I could tell by the fact that even the children in the way-way back were silent. I had given up on playful banter, trying to reason with my youngest, or attempting to cajole anyone in favor of simply driving the car safely: we were on a winding back road with no streetlights and lots of mist after the day of rain. I reached back to put my hand on my middle son's knee, shoring him up for what I was sure was an especially unpleasant task for him.

My youngest was still carrying on; I was concerned that he was going to hyperventilate, and might not be the only one. I glanced in the rear view mirror to see one of our friends nervously leaning as far away from the wrestling duo as possible, looking panic-stricken.

"God, just let me get to a safe place to pull over," I prayed.

Just when our collective crisis was reaching a crescendo, I saw the school crossing sign. I pulled into the school driveway. "Okay, everybody out," I ordered, "let's take a break!"

As the car doors opened, the pressure dissipated. The three oldest boys took off hooting and hollering like banshees into the dark night, down the driveway towards the school parking lot. The others followed not far behind. I sat with my youngest and just held him and rocked him until he stopped crying. Neither of us said anything.

Then: "Honey, your brother and I love you very much. That's why we want you to wear your seatbelt."

"I know, Mommy."

Before we all got back in the car, I thanked my middle son.

"He's such a baby sometimes!"

"Yes, you're right, he *was* acting small…and thank you for not calling him that."

My boys can be thick as thieves or wish they "didn't even have a brother!" Yet often when I insert my presence into their disputes, they turn on me: "Don't you put my brother in time out! You're a mean mom!" Never mind that this boy could have been getting whacked, kicked, poked, looked at the wrong way or otherwise taunted moments before by the very one he is now protecting.

Their verbal game of king of the mountain began from the moment they could form complete sentences.

"I have a cack-u-layta, you-ooh-ooh doh-ohn't!" my oldest had said to his younger brother, long before my youngest came along and certainly before either of them knew what a calculator was.
"Ma ma ma ma…I wanna cack-u-layta!"
"But you-ooh-ooh doh-ohn't!" his brother reminded him.
"Ma ma ma ma…wuzzah cack-u-layta?"

Not long after that, I had said, "Boys, look at the excavator!"

"Where?" they both perked up in their car seats.

"Look out the window on the passenger side!" (where my youngest at the time was sitting.)

"Oh, wow!"

"I can't see it!"

"Nah nah neh nahnah, you dih dint thee it!" Revenge was sweet.

Today the three of them are constantly scrapping to see who can do even the most mundane things first! Better! Faster!

"I win!"

"No, I win!"

"No, I do!"

"No, me!"

"Nuh uh!"

"Uh huh!"

"Yessah!"

"Nossah!"

Repeat.

Repeat.

Repeat with physical contact for emphasis.

My oldest has become sophisticated in verbal sparring. Unctuously, he'll ask, "You don't mean *me,* do you, mom?" in reply to my "I think I'll go nuts of you boys don't stop _____ (fill in the blank)!"

Or rather than saying, "I wish you were never born!" (which my middle still says to my youngest), my oldest will say — so all can hear, "Mom, what do you think it would be like if I were an only child?"

Early on, I did have twinges of guilt over how I could "ruin" my oldest's life by having more children or how could I shove my middle out of the nest by having another baby. Then I'd recall something my mother once told me: "One of the best things you can give your child is a sibling." Indeed, having my second and third sons made it clear to me that when there are more people to love, love is multiplied, not divided.

The love of God flows easily through my boys. For example, my middle son, as a baby, every morning when I lifted him out of his crib would press his face against mine almost until it hurt, eyes boring into mine soulfully, mouth open against my nose, razor-sharp teeth grazing my skin as he lovingly stroked *my* back. At night he would cling so tightly that I could use both hands to get his toothbrush ready after bath without having to put him down.

At age two, he'd bowl over his older brother in a jubilant embrace. From beneath the sprawl, I'd hear a muffled, but not really wholehearted, complaint, "Too much love, Baby, too much!"

And now to his younger brother, "I'm *never* gonna let go of you no matter what!"

This is why — though we're still working on not saying it — I know deep down they don't mean the "H" word. Brotherly love appears to be a special kind of adoration; the kind where there's room for both (inhale) "I *hate* you" and (exhale) "Wanna play D.S. download?"

❧ What Would Grandma Say?

"I sure do miss Grandma!"
"I do, too, honey."

"Mommommom! Remember Grandma?"
"Yes, of course I do!"

"I wah-ah-ahnt my Gra-ah-ah-ma!"
"So do I, love, so do I…"

These are all things my youngest has said at least on a weekly basis during the past year: the first two being matter of fact and cheerful and usually followed up by a fun or funny story, the last reminiscent of Grandma's memorial service, the Saturday after Thanksgiving last year.

He was three at the time and had cried himself to sleep while sitting on the lap of one of his preschool teachers who had come to the service. Today he cries for his Grandma when he is indignant over something his brothers have done, looking for a second opinion about a consequence I've doled out, or just plain tired.

Grandma had become a more or less constant presence in our lives for the almost-year prior to her passing, when she had moved back from California to be near her "grandboybies."

And now a year after her death, she was still that steady presence. Just about every night my middle son asked for "meditations" — bed-time recordings Grandma had made, which I had transferred from cassette tape to CD, not only so each boy would have his own copy, but also so we'd have a back-up source.

We all still talked about her as if she had gone on a long weekend trip somewhere and left us behind, in a collective huff that we didn't get to go.

There were times that I'd spontaneously snap a picture with my cell phone camera of the kids doing something that only Grandma would appreciate — like my youngest eating Froot Loops® with his toes — and then delete it because I had no one to send it to, my heart feeling empty as I confirmed "yes, delete photo" and watched the clock icon ticking as the picture evaporated into nothingness.

Hardly a day passed that one of us didn't muse, "What would Grandma say?" or "Grandma would be so proud of you!"

"Well, she is, Mom!" my oldest reminded me. "Don't you think she can see us from heaven?"

"Well, yes, of course, honey, I suppose she can…"

We celebrated Grandma's birthday in late October with orange-frosted cupcakes. A couple of my best friends brought or sent me flowers and several others sent me notes to commemorate Grandma. Some of us wore her jewelry or flowers in our hair.

"Why did Grandma have to die!?" my middle son demanded.

"I don't know, angel, but if we keep her in our thoughts and prayers, she is alive in us and alive in heaven, right?"

I often wondered, *where is heaven, exactly?* Is it possible that it is right here among us? We can't see or hear everything in the electromagnetic spectrum; in fact the portion that we can see and hear with our human eyes and ears is just a small percentage including certain colors of light and radio waves. We can feel some things that we can't see, such as infra-red light. Perhaps Grandma really is here with us sometimes. Would that explain the sensation that she's standing beside me or the dreams I have about her, or my youngest telling me that he talked to Grandma on the phone last week? Or how sometimes my friends will pass messages from her ("Your mom doesn't like that pumpkin") or say things to me that only she has ever said ("Well, my dear…") in precisely the same tone of voice.

"I can't wait to go to heaven!" my youngest told me.

"Oh, I can wait — I'd miss you too much!" I wondered if Grandma missed us the way we missed her, or if "missing" was just a one way street.

"Well, not if you're already there!" he pointed out.

"Oh, but I'm not ready to go there, little dude. I can wait!"

"I'm not afraid to die," my oldest chimed in."

Is that just what all people under 30 say or is he truly unafraid of the unknown? Because I am not looking forward to dying any time soon, personally. I've had to fight off tendencies toward hypochondria during the past year. I cling fast to the reminder one of my friends told me, "When it's your time, it's your time," imagining that it can't possibly be yet since I don't feel like I am done here, though deep down, I know that's not really up to me.

At a basketball scrimmage one time, another mom relayed the story about her seatmate on an airplane who told her she'd had a brain aneurism, died, gone to heaven, and came back as doctors resuscitated her body. In heaven she had seen her father, and he told her he loved her, that it was not yet her time, and that he would see her when she died again. The mom said that this woman now lived peacefully, unafraid, and with a spirit of gratitude.

Grandma, too, lived her life peacefully, unafraid, and with a spirit of gratitude. I hope and pray that when it is my time, I feel the same way. After all, isn't dying a form of rebirth? Isn't tomorrow just a big unknown, anyway? Would the eternal aspect of heaven make it seem that our time on earth was just a "long weekend"?

Will all our questions be answered when we die?

Still, I can wait.

ᔖ Vaya Con Dios

"I thought I had all the controls in place," she lamented. My friend and I were having coffee and she had mentioned her high-school aged sons' "inappropriate" internet behavior.

I didn't ask specifically what was inappropriate. I was still at the stage where I was mostly dealing with silly and annoying songs on Youtube. I had to endure the likes of Charlie the Unicorn or the Potter Puppet Pals incessantly, which is what I got for insisting the kids use the laptop in public areas of the house, I imagine.

Though, one time, one of my older two asked me for my email address so that an online game site could send him a user name and password validation link. I came over to the kitchen table and had a look. The form he was filling out listed his birthday with a date in 1996. "You typed in the wrong year for your birthday," I informed him.

"No, I did that on purpose, Mom. You have to be at least 13 to play this game."

"But you're not 13."

"I know, but so-and-so plays this game and he's a year younger than me!"

"Do you think so-and-so's mom knows this?"

"Uhmmm…I dunno…"

"Do you think it's okay to lie about your age?"

"Well, no, Mom. But it's only a game, everyone does it."

"No, not everyone does it. You're not gonna do it."

"But Mom!"

"It's not like we've never discussed this. You signed an internet acceptable-use policy for school. Shouldn't the same rules apply here? When you sign something like that, it means you agree — you give your word, your promise!"

"Awww, Mom!"

His feigned outrage was obviously half-hearted.

I don't think anyone (but my youngest) is really in such a hurry to grow up — not long ago they all insisted that an animated movie featuring falsetto-voiced rodents was the absolute only thing they would see albeit the several other choices at the cineplex. Because it was sold out, we traipsed to another theater, and even though the movie was even more annoying than any of their Youtube videos, it made me happy to know that they didn't want anything more sophisticated.

I told my friend, "Imagine if you kept your kids sheltered from MTV, the Internet…never let them go to the movies or the mall…just imagine what would happen when they left home for college, or whatever…"

She rolled her eyes. "I can't even think of it."

A few days later, I was reviewing the Boy Scouts of America's anti-drug pamphlet with my oldest. I cringed at the amount of detail about huffing common household chemicals or overdosing on medicine cabinet staples like pain relievers or decongestant. I recalled the last time I was doing my nails how one of my sons had told me he liked the smell of nail polish remover.

"Put that bottle down, honey, you don't want to inhale any vapors" — *or did he?*

The childproof bottle caps on the acetaminophen and cold medicine don't stop any of the children in my house. "I'll get it, Mom," my youngest said when I asked him if he could just hang on a few minutes.

"Oh, no you won't, honey — you're not old enough to do that!"

"Yes, I am, Mom. I'm four and a *half,* now!" A study in worlds colliding, he struts around with his hand-me-down Nintendo "DeeYesssss!" with his lovey slung over his shoulder à la Linus of the Peanuts gang.

One of our jobs as parents is to grow our children into fully functioning, self-supporting adults. One day they're going to be on their own, so I suppose they have to have some knowledge about what's wrong, in contrast with what's right. Similarly, how are they going to learn conflict resolution if there's never a conflict? (This must be the reason Santa brought only one Wii controller to our house this Christmas.) And how do we learn patience, if we never have opportunities in which to practice it? (I have stopped praying for patience; surely I am blessed with ample opportunities already.)

Of course we try to protect our kids the best we can, but the reality is they have to leave the house sooner or later. You let them go and you hope that they remember the things you've taught them: say "please" and "thank you," look both ways, love God and love your neighbor, change your socks and underwear, count your blessings, clear your plate, just say no to drugs, brush your teeth…

I let go and let God a little bit every day when they go to school. *Vaya con Dios, boys,* I pray silently, as the bus pulls away. *Go with God.*

www.CarolinePoser.com